One Stitch Quilting

the basics

Donna Dewberry and Cindy Casciato

Published by

700 East State Street • Iola, WI 54990-0001
715-445-2214 • 888-457-2873

Our toll-free number to place an order or obtain a free catalog is (800) 258-0929.

Library of Congress Catalog Number: 2005935072

ISBN-10: 0-89689-318-9
ISBN-13: 978-0-89689-318-4

Designed by Emily Adler
Edited by Susan Sliwicki

Printed in China

Acknowledgments

Many people have made this book possible.

Thanks to Julie Stephani, acquistions; Susan Sliwicki, editor; Robert Best, photographer; and Emily Adler, designer. All were instrumental in orchestrating the production of this book at Krause Publications.

Springs Industries was invaluable for providing the fabrics and the support behind the vision.

We are especially indebted to Sue Hausmann and Viking Sewing Machines Inc. for their support and creative input. Sue has inspired us both with her enthusiasm for keeping the world sewing and her tireless energy to help newcomers in the industry.

Special thanks go to: Jill Repp at June Tailor; Dawn Pereira at The Warm Company; Karen Diehl at Prym Consumer USA Inc.; and Fred and Joyce Drexler at Sulky for their continued support of our One Stitch Certification Program and their encouragement to pursue our creative vision.

Dedication

We dedicate this book to Rebekah Stewart of Springs Creative Products. She has worked tirelessly behind the scenes providing us both with encouragement, support and her wise counsel. We are so thankful to count her as a friend, and we want her to know that she is truly a blessing in our lives.

Introduction

Quilting is a shared passion for co-authors (from left) Cindy Casciato and Donna Dewberry.

Designing and making quilts is a creative outlet that allows us to express our personal tastes.

The One Stitch theory of quilting is simple: Have twice the fun in half the time! One Stitch combines the basic processes of piecing and appliqué with quilting to eliminate many of the steps involved in traditional patchwork.

In this book, we share our One Stitch techniques that combine the art of piecing and appliqué with the finishing quilting stitch. We believe that a lifetime skill such as quilting can enrich your life and bring many hours of enjoyment.

There is no ¼" piecing in One Stitch. Instead, folded strips overlap on top of a preprinted fusible grid, or squares and triangles are fused onto a foundation square.

There is no need to piece the top before quilting, either. Strips are stitched down with a basic straight or zigzag stitch. Because those stitches go right through the batting and backing, the quilting gets done at the same time. A fold-over backing completes the outside edges of all but the largest projects with a final border and faux binding.

Compare the ease and speed of One Stitch quilting with traditional quilting.

Traditional Quilting Method	One Stitch Quilting Method
1. Rotary cut the strips and pieces.	1. Rotary cut the strips and pieces.
2. Stitch all of the pieces together with a precise ¼" seam.	2. Cut out the grid. Place it on top of the batting.
3. Stitch the pieces into blocks.	3. Place the batting and grid on top of the backing fabric.
4. Join the blocks into rows, and join the rows to form the quilt top.	4. Lay out the fabric blocks and strips on the grid. Press to hold the pieces in place.
5. Add borders to the quilt top.	5. Zigzag stitch through all of the layers to piece and quilt at the same time.
6. Layer the quilt top with batting and backing.	6. Done.
7. Quilt through the layers.	7. Done.
8. Make a binding.	8. Done.
9. Join the binding to the top of the quilt.	9. Done.
10. Stitch the binding down to the back of the quilt.	10. Done.

In Part 1 of this book, you will learn about the tools and techniques you need to master the One Stitch methods. We know that many of you are accomplished quilters, but some of you are just beginning to quilt. Most of our ideas are vastly different from the traditional methods you may already know, so prepare to be surprised, as there is always more than one way to accomplish your task.

In Part 2, you will practice these techniques with a variety of projects for your home and your wardrobe. Whether you keep these projects for yourself or share them with your family and friends, we hope you find inspiration and enjoyment in the creative process.

Part 2 also provides you with additional tools for your One Stitch journey — patterns to go with the projects, an extensive glossary of terms that's sure to teach even seasoned quilters some new information, and a comprehensive list of Contributors and Resources to help you find all of the same handy tools and supplies we used in this book.

As you layer, arrange and stitch your way through the projects in this book, you may discover that you love the One Stitch method of quilting so much that you want to teach it to others. We'd love to have you join us! Learn more about our One Stitch Instructor Certification Program by visiting our Web site at http://www.onestitchquilting.com.

About the Authors

Donna Dewberry loves anything to do with decorating, painting and crafting. She is best known for her work in decorative painting as a frequent guest on QVC, author of numerous how-to books and host of her own PBS TV show, "One-Stroke Painting With Donna Dewberry."

Donna also authored "Quilting With Donna Dewberry," designed a variety of fabrics for Springs Industries Inc., and appeared on the PBS TV show "America Sews."

A wife, mother of seven, grandmother and native Floridian, Donna resides in Clermont, Fla.

Cindy Casciato is a designer, teacher, author and avid quilter.

She has taught quilting and related topics to numerous guilds and organizations for more than 25 years, including her longtime role as national education manager for Jo-Ann Fabrics.

In addition to co-creating the One Stitch quilting method with Donna Dewberry, Cindy founded Quiltescape, a quilting retreat held annually since 1994.

Her first book, "Block Explosion," was released in 2004. Cindy resides in Ravenna, Ohio.

Table of Contents

Tools and Techniques

Part 1

It doesn't matter whether you've inherited your grandma's trusty sewing machine or you've splurged on brand-new, state-of-the-art everything. If your tools don't work right, you won't, either.

Make sure your sewing machine is in good repair. Have it serviced regularly, follow the maintenance guidelines in your owner's manual, and change your sewing machine needles as needed. In addition to a sewing machine, you'll need a variety of tools and supplies to complete the projects in this book. We've shown the supplies that have worked well for our methods; see Contributors and Resources for details. Choose the tools that work best for you.

Tools and Supplies

Sewing and Quilting

Sewing machine

Additional machine accessories, including walking foot, spare bobbins and spare needles

Seam ripper

Thread

Fabric

Cotton batting

Computer with color printer and compatible fabric sheets to print your own photos to fabric

Cutting

45 mm rotary cutter and spare blades

28 mm rotary cutter and spare blades

Nonskid grip for rotary cutting ruler and mat

6" x 24" clear rotary cutting ruler

4" x 14" clear rotary cutting ruler

12½" square clear rotary cutting ruler

Clear ruler specifically made for cutting edge patterns on fleece

18" x 24" rotary cutting mat

6½" fabric scissors

Ergonomic thread snips

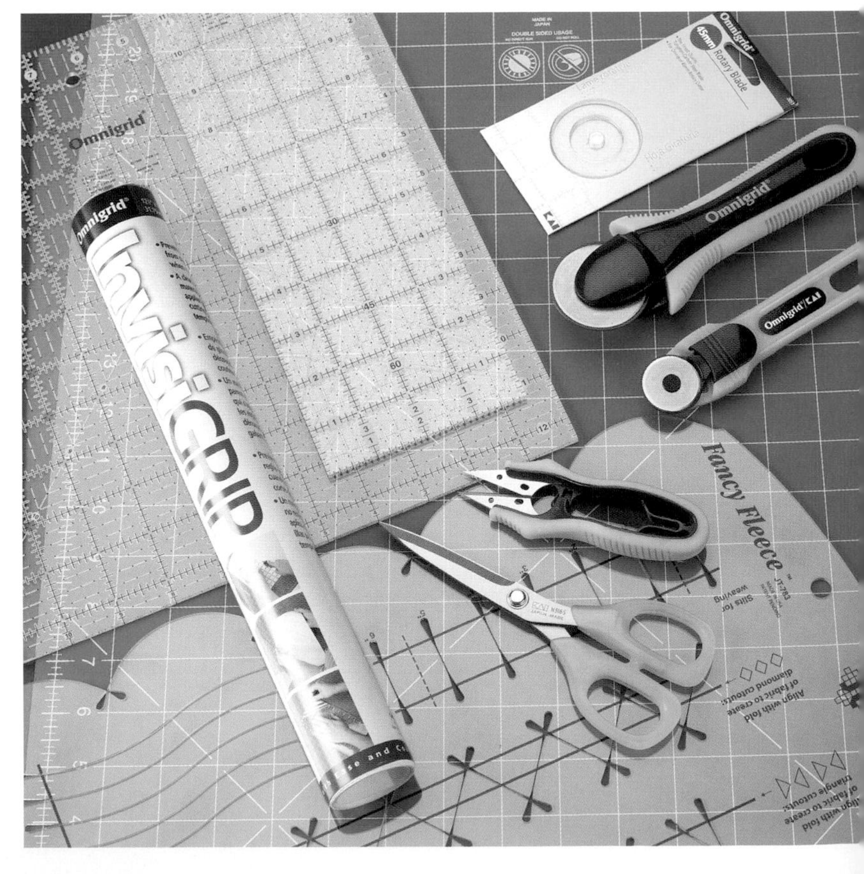

Pinning and Basting

Glass-head straight pins
Curved basting pins
Sewing/craft glue stick
Quilt basting spray
Temporary spray adhesive
Pincushion

Marking

Fine-line permanent fabric marking pen
Quilter's pencil
Fabric eraser
Marking pen or pencil
Tailor's chalk pencil

Pressing and Fusing

Iron

Ironing board or sewing station/organizer

Quilter's pressing bars

Finger presser and/or bamboo stiletto

Fusible tape in varying widths, including ½" and ⅝"

Fusible web

Fusible quilt top grid marked in 1" increments

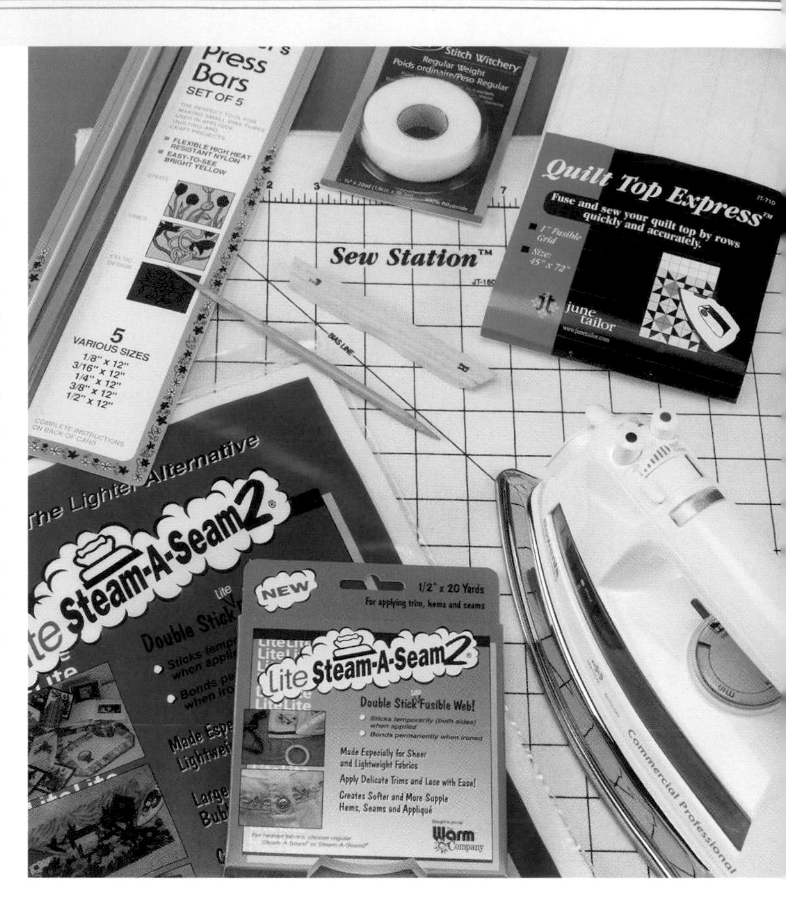

Embellishing

Chenille bias strips

Chunky yarn

Rickrack

Ribbon

Other trims as desired

General Techniques

Rotary Cutting

It takes a little practice to get the hang of rotary cutting. Practice your technique on a yard of muslin before you dive into your project fabrics. Make several cuts until all of your strips are cut accurately.

Use rotary cutters with care; these super-sharp cutters can slice through fingers as easily as they do fabrics. Always engage the blade guard when you finish cutting to protect both you and the blade. Avoid using a back-and-forth sawing motion with the blade; this can cause serious injury.

Keep your cutting as accurate as possible by avoiding common pitfalls. Limit how many layers you try to cut at a time, because fabrics can shift within the layers and cause your cuts to vary. If you didn't get a clean cut, start at the bottom of the ruler and roll through the fabric again, in case you failed to use enough pressure the first time. If that doesn't work, though, replace the rotary cutter's blade to ensure clean cuts.

Most of the strips needed for the projects in this book are cut on the crosswise grain, across the width of the fabric. There may be times when a border must be cut on the lengthwise grain, parallel to the selvage, to take advantage of the additional length of the yardage.

Cutting on the Crosswise Grain

1. Fold the length of the fabric in half, bringing the selvage edges together. The bottom fold should be straight and free of puckers. Beware: Sometimes the selvages will not align perfectly.

2. Square up one end of the fabric so that it's at a 90-degree angle to the selvage-to-selvage fold.

3. Place the folded fabric on your rotary mat so that the bottom fold is on a crosswise line near the bottom edge of the mat, and the side of the fabric to be squared is on your left. Allow the raw edges of the fabric to extend across a vertical line.

4. Place the 6" x 24" ruler across the folded edge of the fabric, near the left edge on the closest vertical line that will cover the raw edge of the fabric. Check to make sure horizontal lines marked on the ruler and the mat are parallel to the folded edge. Place your fingertips on the ruler. Firmly press down, and extend your pinky to the outside edge of the ruler to brace it. Avoid placing your fingers across the ruler in the path of the cutter.

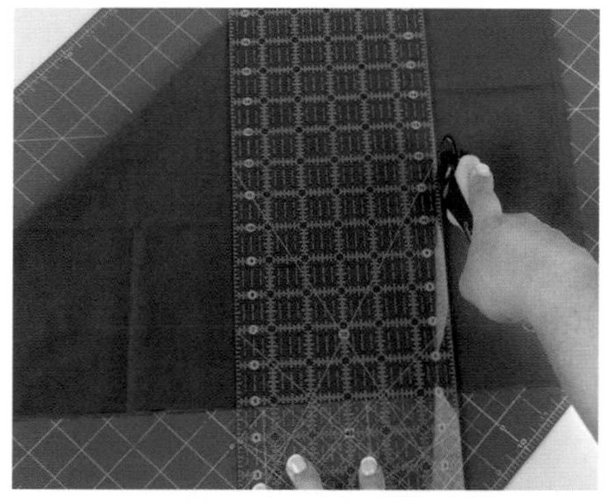

5. Tap the flat side of your blade against the bottom edge of the ruler. Push the rotary cutter firmly against the ruler, rolling through from the bottom edge of the fabric up to the top.

6. Cut the strips required for your project. For instance, if you need a 3" strip, align the 3" mark on the ruler with the left edge of the fabric. Align a horizontal line near the bottom of the ruler with the fold. Before each cut, make sure that both edges of the fabric align with vertical and horizontal markings on the ruler. If they don't, square up the fabric again before cutting more strips. If a strip has a bend in the middle, it means the left edge of the fabric was not at a 90-degree angle. Square the fabric up before cutting again.

Pressing

When it comes to quilting, there are few matters more pressing than how you wield your iron.

Pressing vs. Ironing

Pressing removes wrinkles and improves cutting and sewing. But don't get pressing confused with its laundry drudge cousin, ironing.

Pressing uses a lifting motion that allows the weight of the iron to flatten the pieces or seams in your projects. It prevents fabrics from stretching. Ironing, on the other hand, uses a sliding motion across the fabric, which can stretch pieces. Iron individual fabrics prior to cutting them into pieces for your quilt projects.

Using Steam

To steam or not to steam? The rules are simple.

Turn the steam on when you:

- Press larger quantities of fabric.
- Adhere appliqués to the background fabrics.
- Apply fusible web tape to fabric strips.

Turn the steam off when you:

- Apply the quilt top grid to the batting.
- Work with fleece.

Pressing the Fusible Quilt Grid

1. Place the grid with the fusible side down on top of the batting.

2. Fuse the grid in place using a dry iron on a medium setting.

3. Hold the iron in place for 10 to 12 seconds, then reposition it. Avoid sliding the iron or using steam, both of which will distort the shape of the grid.

4. Spray the top of the grid with an adhesive. This will create a surface similar to a sticky note on top of the grid, which will allow fabrics to cling to the grid until they are permanently sewn down through the top, batting and backing. We like to use Sulky's KK 2000 Temporary Spray Adhesive, which allows fabric pieces to be repositioned on top of the grid.

One Stitch Basics

A variety of elements work together to make the One Stitch technique so quick, easy and fun. Here are detailed looks at the blocks, strips, finishes and embellishments that are used to create the projects in this book. Be sure to mark this section for your easy reference; it will come in handy as you work on the projects.

A materials list accompanies the step-by-step instructions for each project. Each list details specific fabrics, patterns, decorative trims and other special supplies used to complete the projects as shown. If you can't find the fabric or trim shown in this book, don't despair! Trust your personal taste to help you choose the right prints, colors and styles that will work best for you.

One Stitch Block Gallery

The block is the basic unit of the quilt top.

The One Stitch method lends itself to many variations of blocks. It also works well with blocks that are irregular in shape and size. Fused patches, appliqué shapes, printed fabric panels, custom photo prints, novelty fabrics, embroidery, stitchery, overlapping strips — a combination of any or all of these components are used to create the blocks used in the One Stitch method.

Traditional piecing is not a part of the One Stitch technique; when patchwork blocks are used, the patches are fused to a background block. The cut size of the block and the finished or final sewn measurement of a completed One Stitch block without seam allowances is indicated in each pattern.

The One Stitch method requires a 1" seam allowance to be added to the finished size of the patchwork or appliquéd block; thus, a finished 9" block would be cut 10" to allow for seam allowances when adding borders, sashing and joining strips.

Following are the types of blocks used to complete the projects in this book. Most of the blocks shown are a finished size of 9" and are interchangeable in any of the projects calling for 9" to 10" blocks. Have fun mixing and matching blocks to get the perfect look for your projects!

Appliqué Block

Cutting Rule: Trace the appliqué shapes onto one side of fusible web paper. Remove the opposite piece of fusible web paper, and place the sticky side of the fusible web on the wrong side of the desired fabric. Steam press the fusible web in place. Cut out the fabric pieces. Remove the second piece of fusible web paper. Place the pieces on the background block as desired to form the design.

Pressing Rule: Press the pieces with a steam iron from the fabric side of the appliqué piece.

Printed Panel Block

Cutting Rule: Cut the blocks from printed fabric panels, such as Springs' Art to Sew Quilt Squares by Donna Dewberry, to fit the measurement required in the pattern. For printed panel blocks, fold the untrimmed block into quarters, making sure the artwork is centered on the fold, and cut the block half of the finished block size from the fold line. For example, if the pattern calls for a 10" cut block, cut the folded block 5" from the fold.

Pressing Rule: Retain the creases from folding the block until you place the block onto the grid/batting; use the creases to align the block.

Cutout Block

CUTTING RULE: Cut double-sided paper-backed fusible web into sections that are large enough to cover the needed fabric pieces. Remove one side of the paper, and place the fusible web sticky side down on the wrong side of the fabric. Steam press the fusible web in place. Cut out the fabric pieces from the right side of the fabric into the shapes and sizes desired. Remove the second piece of paper from the fusible web. Place the cutouts on the background block to form the design.

PRESSING RULE: Use an iron on a steam setting to press the piece from the fabric side of the cutout piece.

Large-Scale or Novelty Fabric Block

CUTTING RULE: Cut the large-scale or novelty fabric into a block shape to represent the space in a pattern that calls for a block. Use the cut size measurement to cut your fabric block.

PRESSING RULE: Press the block in half, and then press it in half again to create the centering crease lines. Use the crease lines to match up to the grid/batting lines when placing the block on the grid.

Photo Block

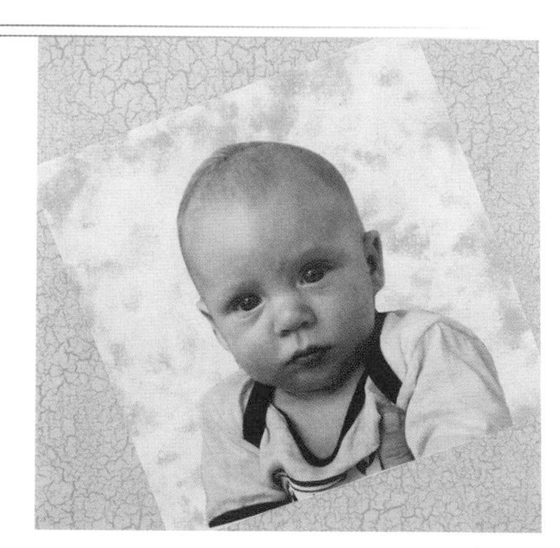

CUTTING RULE: Cut out the photo from printed photo fabric, and cut it to the size required by the pattern.

PRESSING RULE: Follow the manufacturer's directions to press photo blocks. As a general rule, avoid using steam. Use a muslin pressing cloth over the top of the printed fabric, or press the piece from the back of the block once it is in place.

Patchwork Blocks

CUTTING RULE: Cut out the background square 1" larger than the finished patchwork block. Cut out the patches without a seam allowance, and place the patches right side up on the sticky side of the fusible web. Follow the cutting size listed in each pattern. Cut out the paper-backed fusible web patchwork pieces. Specific directions follow to create the Butterfly, Tilted Square Photo, Tulip, Crazy Patch and Nine-Patch Star blocks.

PRESSING RULE: Press the background square in half, and then press it in half again to create the centering crease lines. Press each patchwork piece to the background square, using the centering lines to ensure proper placement.

Butterfly Block

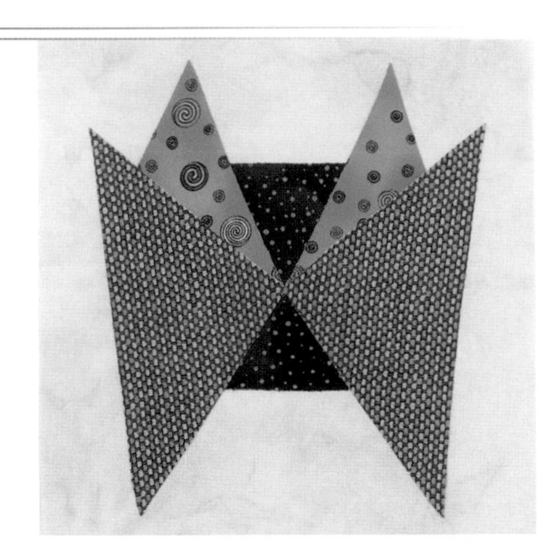

Materials

- 1/3 yd. cream sponge print
- 1/4 yd. fusible web
- 3/16 yd. orange print
- 1/8 yd. brown print
- 1/8 yd. turquoise print
- Chasing Butterflies Wall Hanging pattern pieces on page 119
- Fusible tape
- Sewing tools and supplies

Fabric	Trace, Fuse and Cut	For
Fusible web	Trace patterns A, B, BR, C and CR on the paper side, then cut out	Butterfly pattern pieces
Brown print	Fuse A, then cut out	A
Turquoise print	Fuse B and BR, then cut out	B, BR
Orange print	Fuse C and CR, then cut out	C, CR
Cream sponge print	1 square, 10" x 10"	Background square

1. Use an erasable marking pen to draw lines across the background square on each diagonal, on the vertical center and on the horizontal center. If you prefer, you can fold the background square and press all of the creases in place.

2. Place each fusible web pattern piece onto the wrong side of the desired fabric. Steam press the pieces in place.

3. Cut out the fabric shapes. Let the pieces cool for 30 seconds, then remove the paper to reveal the tacky surface of the fusible web.

4. Place the pattern pieces wrong side down on top of the background square in their alphabetical order, starting with A. Center A on the block by matching the crease lines in the block. Fuse A in place. Add the remaining pieces following the alphabetical pattern order. Fuse each piece in place.

Tilted Square Photo Block

Materials

- 1/3 yd. green sponge or batik print
- 8½" x 11" sheet of photo printable fabric
- Computer and printer
- Fusible tape
- 1 yd. rickrack or bulky yarn trim
- Sewing tools and supplies

Fabric	Cut	For
Green sponge	1 square, 10" x 10"	Background square
Printed photo	1 square, 8" x 8"	Photo square

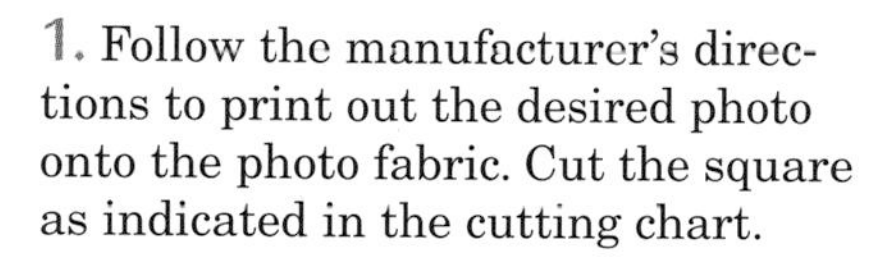

1. Follow the manufacturer's directions to print out the desired photo onto the photo fabric. Cut the square as indicated in the cutting chart.

2. Place fusible tape under each of the four corners of the photo square. Fuse the photo square as desired to the background square.

3. Sew the purchased trim to the edges of the finished block before placing it on the grid. This will save a lot of time and make the quilting process go much faster.

Tulip Block

Materials

- 1/3 yd. purple crackle print
- 1/16 yd. green crackle print
- 1/16 yd. violet petals print
- 1/16 yd. pink crackle print
- ¼ yd. double-sided fusible web
- Fusible tape
- Sewing tools and supplies

Fabric	Cut	For
Green crackle	1 square, 2" x 2"	Leaves
Violet petals	1 square, 2" x 2"	Envelope rose
Pink crackle	2 squares, 2" x 2"	Tulip petals
Purple crackle	1 square, 10" x 10"	Background square

1. Use an erasable marking pen to draw lines across the background square on each diagonal, on the vertical center and on the horizontal center. If you prefer, you can fold the background square and press all of the creases in place.

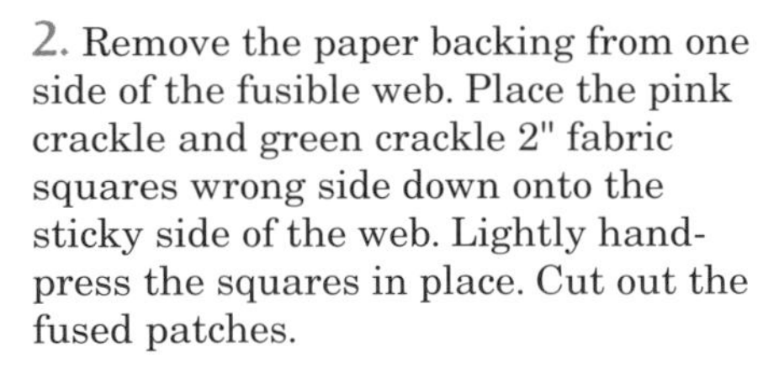

2. Remove the paper backing from one side of the fusible web. Place the pink crackle and green crackle 2" fabric squares wrong side down onto the sticky side of the web. Lightly hand-press the squares in place. Cut out the fused patches.

3. Cut one pink crackle square once on the diagonal. Cut one green square once on the diagonal.

4. Pull the backing paper off of all the patches. Starting in the center of the background block, match the corners of the pink crackle square with the crease marks on the background square. Lightly hand press the patch in place.

5. Fold the violet petals square in half diagonally, wrong sides together.

6. Bring the right point from the folded triangle to the bottom point of the triangle. Finger press in place.

7. Repeat Step 6 for the left point. Position the folded piece at the top of the pink crackle square.

8. Continue to add patches around the center square to form the tulip shape.

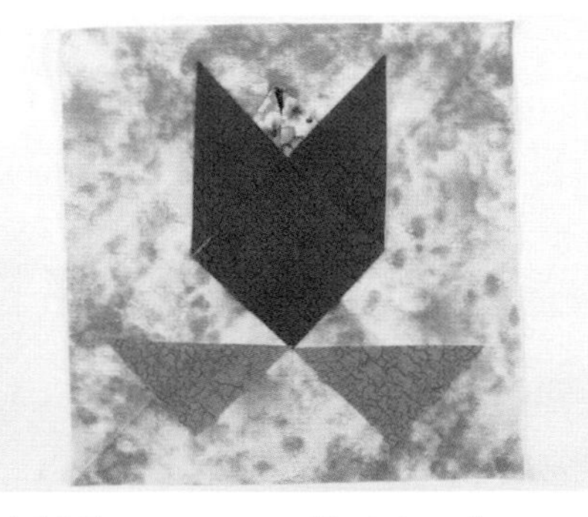

9. Add the green crackle triangles to form the leaves. Steam press the patches to the background square to complete the block.

Crazy Patch Block

Materials

- ½ yd. purple fern print
- ⅛ yd. purple crackle print
- ¼ yd. violet small floral print
- ¼ yd. pink crackle print
- ⅛ yd. green fern print
- ⅓ yd. green crackle print
- ⅛ yd. green sponge print
- Crazy Patch Purse pattern pieces on pages 120 and 121
- Sewing tools and supplies

Fabric	Cut	For
Purple crackle	1 rectangle, 4¼" x 7½" 1 rectangles, 7" x 8"	A H
Violet floral	1 rectangles, 3¼" x 7½" 1 rectangles, 5½" x 6"	B J
Pink crackle	1 rectangles, 5" x 6½" 1 rectangles, 6¾" x 7½"	C I
Green fern	1 rectangles, 4½" x 5½"	D
Green crackle	1 rectangles, 5¼" x 6½" 1 rectangles, 6" x 7"	E G
Green sponge	1 rectangles, 4½" x 7¼"	F
Purple fern*	1 rectangle, 15" x 18"*	Backing fabric*

NOTE: The directions for this block will create a rectangular block, such as is used for the Crazy Patch Purse. To make a square block, change the size of the background rectangle to 10" x 10", use only pattern pieces A, B, C, D, E and F, and lay the patches out to fit accordingly.

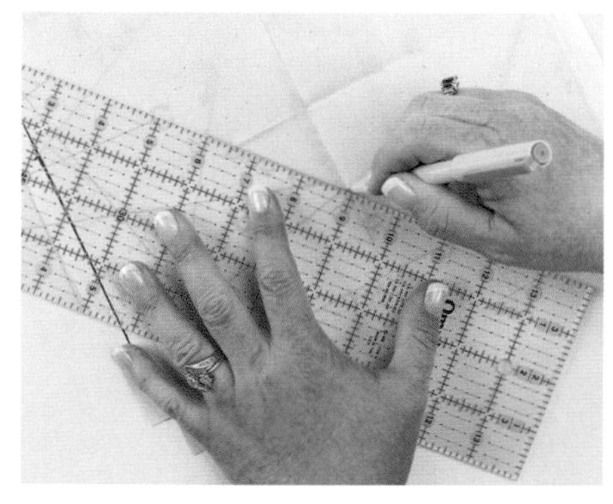

1. Use a permanent ink fabric marker to transfer the Crazy Patch pattern to the quilt top grid.

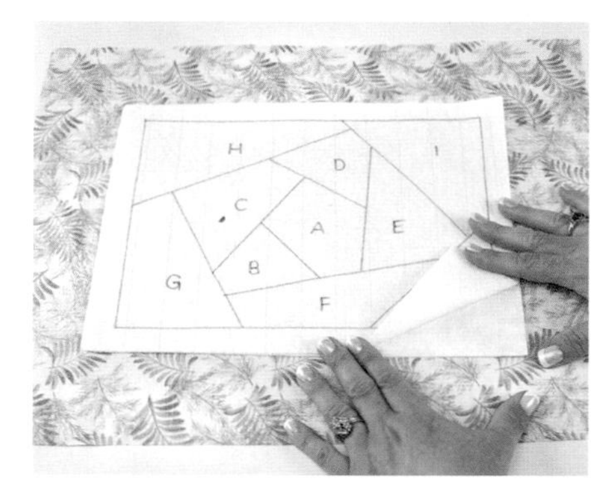

2. Using an iron on a medium setting, press the quilt top grid to the batting. Steam press the grid/batting to the interfacing. Center the grid/batting/ interfacing sandwich on the backing fabric.

3. Fold the strips cut for pattern pieces A through J in half lengthwise. Press each piece to turn each into a single-fold strip. For each strip, apply temporary spray adhesive to the inside the fabric, and finger press the layers together.

4. Place a small strip of fusible tape on one side of the outside of each strip. Starting with A, place each strip in place on the grid according to the pattern. Piece A can be placed on the pattern in any direction so long as it overlaps all lines.

5. Continue to add pieces in alphabetical order. As you position each piece, make sure that the folded edge of the fabric strip is on the pattern line. Adjust the pieces to cover any raw edges that may be exposed.

6. Once you are satisfied with the layout, press the pieces in place. Trim away any excess fabric from the edge of the batting.

Nine-Patch Star Block

Materials

- 1/8 yd. purple crackle print
- 1/8 yd. pink crackle print
- 1/8 yd. lime crackle print
- 1/8 yd. violet fern print
- 1/3 yd. green sponge print
- Sewing tools and supplies

Fabric	Cut	For
Purple crackle	10 squares, 3" x 3"	Folded triangles
Pink crackle	1 square, 3" x 3"	Center triangles
Lime crackle	1 square, 3" x 3"	Center square
Violet fern	3 squares, 3" x 3"	Side and accent triangles
Green sponge	1 square, 10" x 10"	Background square

1. Use an erasable marking pen to draw lines across the background square on each diagonal, on the vertical center and on the horizontal center. If you prefer, you can fold the background square and press all of the creases in place.

2. Remove the paper backing from one side of the fusible web. Place two purple, one pink, one lime and three violet fern fabric squares wrong side down on the sticky side of the web. Lightly hand press the patches in place. Cut out the patches, then steam press each patch from the paper side of the fusible web.

3. Cut one pink, one violet fern and two purple squares twice on the diagonal to yield quarter-square triangles. Cut two violet fern squares once on the diagonal to yield half-square triangles. Remove the paper backing from all of the patches.

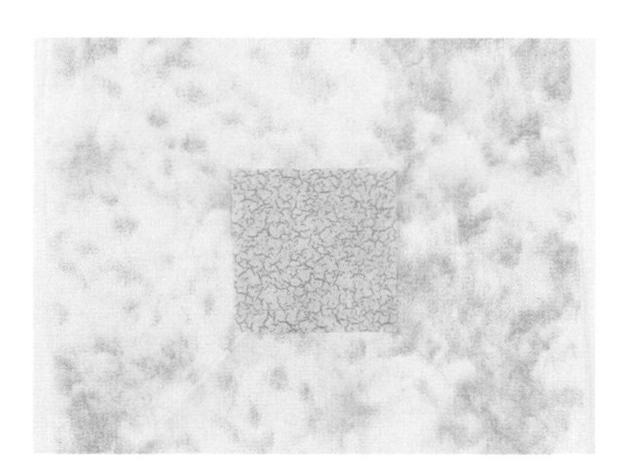

◀ 4. Starting in the center of the background block, match the corners of the lime center square with the crease or ink marks as shown. Lightly hand press the patch in place.

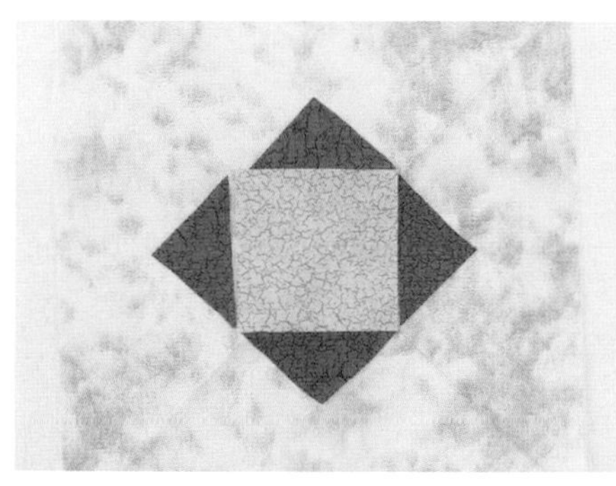

5. Continue to add patches around the center square, starting with the pink quarter-square triangles.

6. Add the purple quarter-square triangles, followed by the green fern triangles.

7. Steam press all of the placed patches to the background to form the nine patch star block.

8. Use the eight remaining purple squares to create eight folded triangles. See One Stitch Embellishments for detailed instructions.

9. Place a folded triangle on top of each fused purple triangle in the nine-patch star block; be sure that each folded triangle faces toward the center square. Use a dab of fabric glue or a small piece of fusible tape to hold each folded triangle in place.

10. Use a zigzag stitch to stitch around all of the patches; be sure to catch all of the patches.

One Stitch Embellishments

Embellishments are a great way to add texture and pizazz to your projects. The following quick and easy techniques take embellishments to the next level by using fabric and yarn to add three-dimensional touches to your pieces.

Folded Rosebud

1. Fold a 2" square of fabric in half diagonally, wrong sides together.

2. Bring the right point from the folded triangle to the bottom point of the triangle. Finger press in place.

3. Repeat Step 3 for the left point of the folded triangle to yield a folded square.

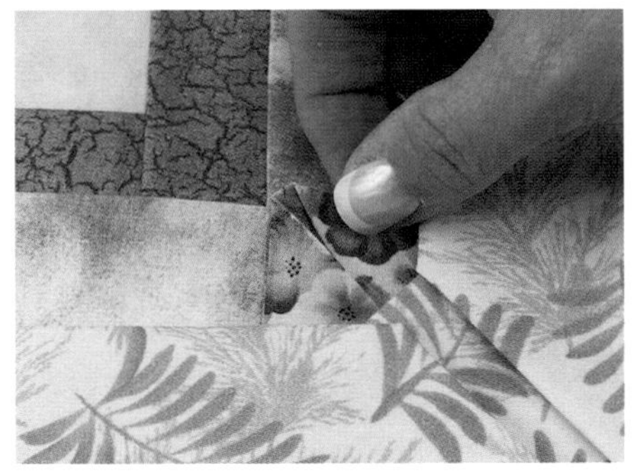

4. Position the folded bud as desired in the piece. Stitch in place.

Envelope Rose

1. Fold a 2" square of fabric in half diagonally, wrong sides together. Bring the right point from the folded triangle to the bottom point of the triangle. Finger press in place. Repeat for the left point of the folded triangle to yield a folded square.

2. Cut the raw edges under the final mitered corner to yield a folded bud.

3. Cut a 2" square of fabric in half diagonally. Place one triangle wrong side up, and position the folded bud as shown.

4. Fold the bottom point of the triangle toward the tip of the folded bud.

5. Fold the side tips of the triangle toward the center of the folded bud.

6. Position the envelope rose as desired in the piece. Stitch in place.

Folded Triangles

1. Fold a 3" x 3" square in half on the diagonal to form a triangle. Press.

2. Fold the triangle created in Step 1 in half again. Press.

3. Lift and fold one corner of the triangle back on top of itself to create a dimensional triangle.

Yarn Loop Trim

1. Loop yarn around a 2"- to 3"-wide strip of cardboard. The longer and more dense you desire the finished loop trim to be, the more loops you need to make.

2. On the last loop, extend the yarn a few extra inches beyond the edge of the cardboard. Cut the yarn, and slip the loops off of the cardboard so they are intact.

3. Position the loops as desired on the piece. Stitch the trim in place along the bottom edge of the loops, making sure your stitches go through each loop.

4. Fluff the finished loops as desired.

One Stitch Strips

The One Stitch Quilting method uses many types of strips. Each project will indicate the type of strip needed, as well as the cut size and whether to cut the strip crosswise or lengthwise.

Rules accompany each type of strip to make it easy to know what to use where. The Usage Rule explains where each strip typically is used. The Cutting Rule details how each strip is cut; it is based upon the finished width of the strip needed and the type of strip required. In most cases, the strip is cut across the width of the fabric; however, strips for larger quilts may need to be cut from the length of the yardage. The Pressing Rule indicates how to make each strip; it includes specific folding and pressing instructions.

Following are the strips you will use to complete the projects in this book.

Single-Fold Strip

Usage Rule: Use a single-fold strip to cover the raw edge of a block, provide an inner border or serve as trim.

Cutting Rule: Cut the strip twice the width of the finished size plus ½" seam allowance.

Pressing Rule: Press the strip in half lengthwise, wrong sides together.

Double-Fold Strip

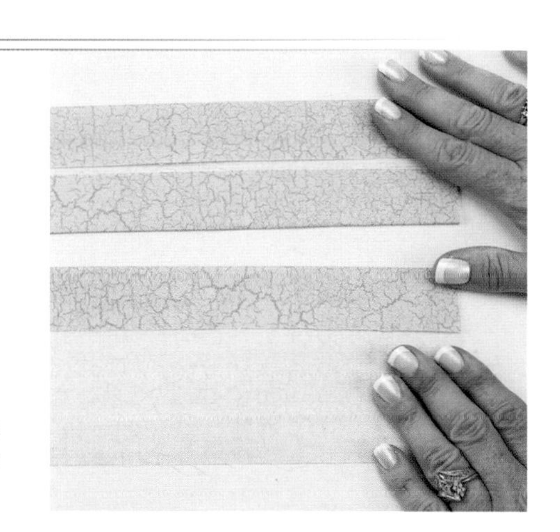

Usage Rule: Use a double-fold strip for sashing between blocks.

Cutting Rule: Cut the strip twice the width of the finished size.

Pressing Rule: Press the strip in half lengthwise, wrong sides together. Reopen the strip, and refold it to bring both raw edges toward the crease line in the middle. This will leave two folded edges on the long sides of the strip, which forms the double-fold strip.

Double-Fold Tuck Strip

Usage Rule: Use a double-fold tuck strip for garments.

Cutting Rule: Cut the strip of fabric four times the width of the finished size plus ½" seam allowance.

Pressing Rule: Press ½"-wide fusible tape to the wrong side of one long edge of the strip. Leave the paper in place. Fold the opposite raw edge in and up to the crease line of the folded edge of the fusible tape fold, which will overlap the opposite raw edge. Press. Fold the strip in half again, and press to complete the strip.

Triple-Fold Strip

USAGE RULE: Use the triple-fold strip for purse or tote bag straps.

CUTTING RULE: Cut the strip of fabric four times the width of the finished size.

PRESSING RULE: Create a double-fold strip. Press the strip in half again to conceal any raw edges.

Quick-Turn Fold Strip

USAGE RULE: Use the quick-turn fold strip for outer borders.

CUTTING RULE: Cut the strip of fabric twice the finished width plus 1¼" seam allowance.

PRESSING RULE: Press the strip in half lengthwise, wrong sides together. Open the strip. Press ½"-wide fusible tape to the long edge on the right side of the fabric. Repeat this step for both sides of the strip. Leave the paper in place. Using the tape as your guide, turn under and press a ½" seam allowance to the wrong side of the strip. Press the strip in half, wrong sides together.

Double-Load Strip

USAGE RULE: Use the quick-turn, double-load strip, which is loaded with two strips of batting, to increase the size of the quilt, usually to add borders to complete a quilt.

CUTTING RULE: Cut the strip of fabric twice the finished width plus 1¼" seam allowance. Cut the first batting strip the width of the pressed strip measured from the center fold up to the ½" fold. Cut the second strip of batting the width of the first strip less ½".

PRESSING RULE: Press following the quick-turn fold strip pressing rule. Load one strip of batting under the ½" seam allowance. Load the second batting strip on top of the first batting strip adjacent to the ½" edge. Slip the ½" edges over the raw edge of the quilt. Remove the paper tape, and steam press the border from the front side of the quilt. Flip the quilt to the back side. Remove the tape, and steam press the border in place.

Miter-Fold Strip

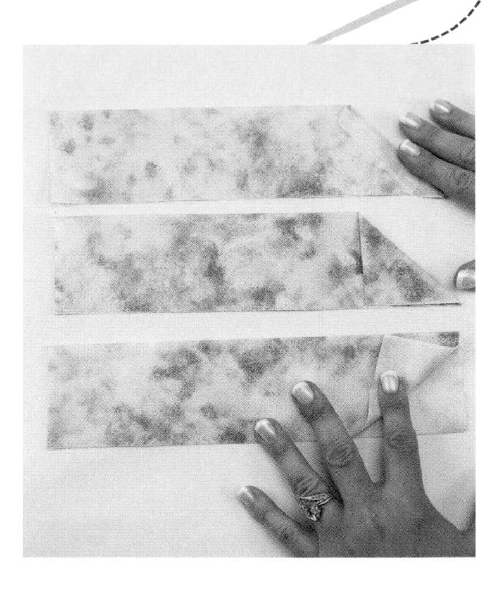

USAGE RULE: Use the miter-fold strip for mitered corners. It eliminates the need to stitch down miters.

CUTTING RULE: Cut the strip twice the width of the finished size plus ½" seam allowance. Overlap two corner strips, and cut the edges even with each other. Repeat this step for all four corners of the quilt.

PRESSING RULE: Press the strip in half lengthwise, placing wrong sides together. Fold under the top strip in each of the four corners of the quilt to form a triangle or 45-degree angle. Press the miter down to crease it. Lift up the new crease; trim the excess fabric ½" away from the new mitered fold. Press a piece of ½"-wide fusible tape to the wrong side of the mitered fold. Remove the paper, and press the miter to the bottom strip.

Trim Strip

USAGE RULE: Trim strips often are used between two borders or between sashing and borders. Trim strips are not stitched down. Ribbon, piping or lace can be used in place of trim strips against the edges of blocks, sashing or borders. This trim doesn't take up space on the grid or increase the overall size of the quilt.

CUTTING RULE: Cut the strip twice the width of the finished size plus ½" seam allowance.

PRESSING RULE: Press the strip in half lengthwise, wrong sides together.

Joining Strip

USAGE RULE: Use joining strips to cover raw edges when joining two sections of a quilt. A joining strip is a single-fold strip that connects two sections of a quilt.

CUTTING RULE: Cut the strip twice the finished size of the sashing plus 1"; this seam allowance is based on the purpose of the strip.

PRESSING RULE: Press the strip in half lengthwise, wrong sides together.

One Stitch Finishes

The One Stitch method of finishing a project is determined by the size and purpose of the project. Double-fold borders or ribbon-fold finishes commonly are used for wall hangings. Larger, lap sized quilts use the add-on finish to complete the borders and final edges of the quilt. Some very simple projects, such as place mats, require a quick-turn finish.

The following finishes are used for the projects in this book; refer to this section for complete instructions as needed.

Single-Fold Border Finish

The single-fold border finish uses fleece to form the final border and finished edge of the quilt, such as in the Quick and Cuddly Fleece Quilt project. Unlike other fabrics, fleece only needs to be folded once, as its edges do not ravel. Avoid pressing fleece; any pressing marks will become permanent.

Tip

Consider using a specialty tool, such as the Fancy Fleece tool by June Tailor, to make decorative edges, such as scallops, on your fleece.

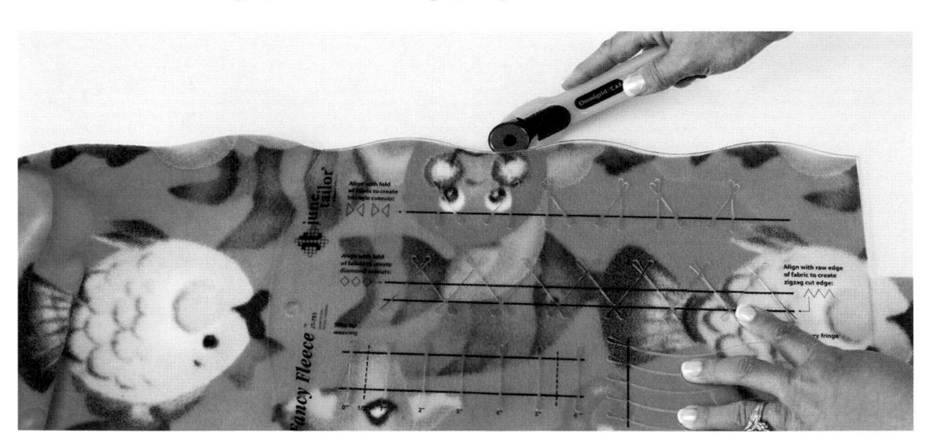

Cutting Guidelines

Follow these cutting guidelines to get single-fold borders of varying sizes on the front of your quilt.

4" BORDER: Add 16" to the panel width and length. Cut a 3½" square from each corner of the fleece.

4½" BORDER: Add 18" to the panel width and length. Cut a 4" square from each corner of the fleece.

5" BORDER: Add 20" to the panel width and length. Cut a 4½" square from each corner of the fleece.

5½" BORDER: Add 22" to the panel width and length. Cut a 5" square from each corner of the fleece.

6 " BORDER: Add 24" to the panel width and length. Cut a 5½" square from each corner of the fleece.

Assemble

1. Cut out the fabric panel.

2. Measure the panel's width and length; in general, most panels are 34" to 36" x 40" to 42". Subtract the width measurement of the panel from the width of the fleece; most fleece fabric is 58" to 60" wide. The difference is the width you need to cut the fleece. Add the difference to the measured length of the panel to determine how long to cut the fleece.

3. From each corner of the fleece, cut a square whose sides are ½" less than the width of the border you desire. Refer to the Single-Fold Border Finish Cutting Guidelines.

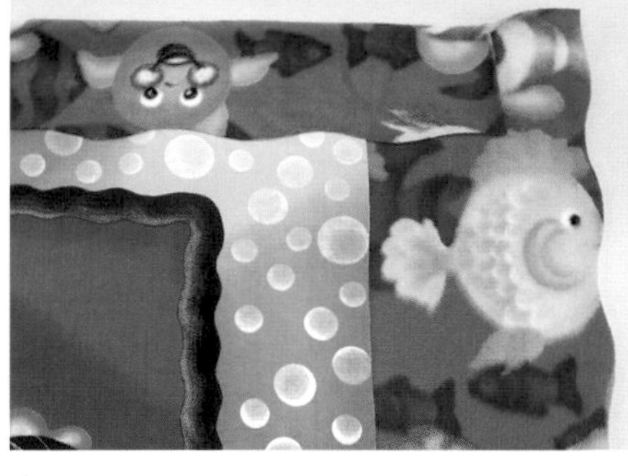

4. Fold the cut edge toward the center panel to the desired width. Stitch in place.

Double-Fold Border Finish

The double-fold border finish technique uses the backing fabric to form the final border and finished edge of your quilt. Press each part of the fold as you go; this will ensure that the final border edge will lay flat for stitching.

Assemble

1. Multiply the desired width of the final border by 4.

2. Measure the batting grid. Add the number determined in Step 1 to both the width and the length of the batting grid, plus a ½" seam allowance. This is the size to cut the backing fabric.

3. Cut the backing fabric to the dimensions determined in Steps 1 and 2.

4. Fold the backing fabric in half twice; press the centering marks. Unfold the backing fabric. Lay it out wrong side up.

5. Center the batting on the backing fabric so there is an equal amount of backing fabric around all four sides of the batting. Take your time with this step; accuracy is key. Measure the outside edges of the backing to ensure the placement is accurate.

6. Fold each corner of the backing fabric up to the edge of batting to form a triangle. Press the crease.

7. Fold under the top of the triangle of the backing fabric to touch the bottom edge of the batting. Press the crease.

8. Fold the outside edge of the backing up to the outside edge of the batting. Fold up the top edge first, then the bottom, left and right edges. Press.

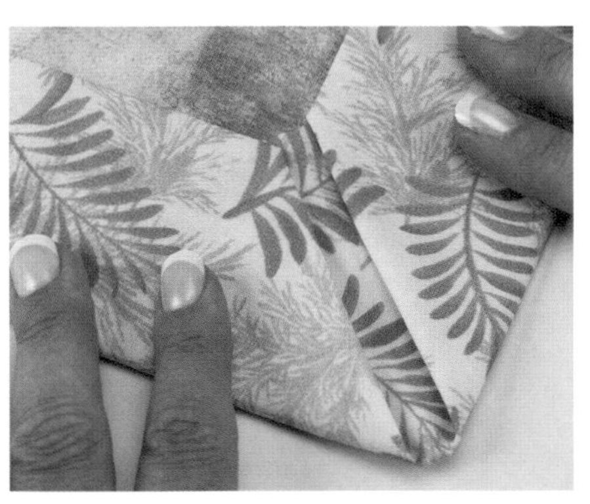

9. Fold up the backing one more time following the same order — top, bottom, side, side — and bring the backing up and over the final border edge of the quilt. The corners will form a square miter.

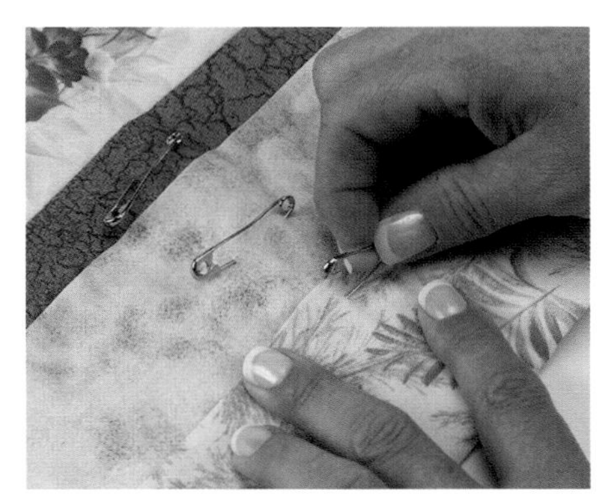

10. Pin the backing in place to hold. Press.

11. If desired, insert folded rosebuds under the border fold to add a three-dimensional embellishment. See One Stitch Embellishments for detailed instructions.

Pillow Back Finish

The double-fold border finish technique uses the backing fabric to form the final border and finished edge of your quilt. Press each part of the fold as you go; this will ensure that the final border edge will lay flat for stitching.

Assemble

1. Cut two rectangles, each 9" x 16".

2. Press under a ½"-wide seam allowance on all four sides of each 9" x 16" rectangle.

3. Press ½"-wide fusible tape along the top edge of all four sides of the first rectangle.

4. Press ½"-wide fusible tape along the top edge of one long side and both short sides of the second rectangle. Press one strip of ½" fusible tape on wrong side of the remaining long side. Remove the paper from the tape.

◀ 5. Place a 12" strip of hook and loop tape on the top long side of one rectangle and on the underside of the other rectangle. These tapes will close the opening of the pillow and overlap each other.

6. Steam press the hook and loop tape in place, then sew it down to secure it. Overlap the two rectangles to form one square. Align the square on the back of the wall hanging; allow the edges of the square to overlap slightly beyond the border fold.

7. Steam press the square to the back of the quilt to hold it in place. Turn the quilt over. Use a zigzag stitch to sew down the folded edge against the last border strip; catch the border fold and pillow backing in one stitch.

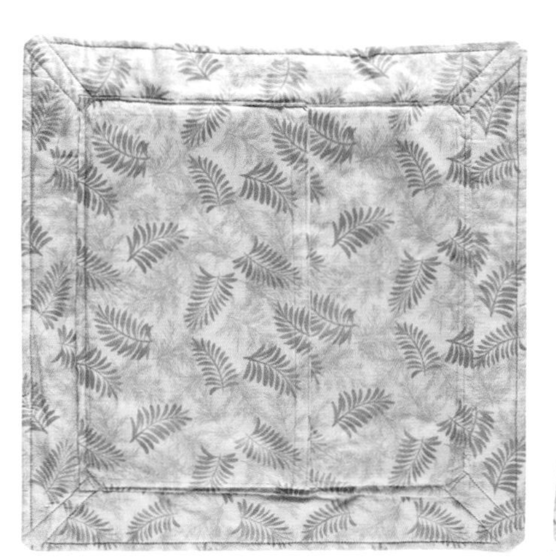

8. Insert a pillow form into the finished pillow.

Ribbon-Fold Finish

The ribbon-fold finish technique incorporates ribbon along the top edge of the final border to provide a decorative alternative to the usual hanging sleeve. While virtually any kind of ribbon will work, you may find it easiest to work with a wire-edged ribbon, which will hold the folds. Stitch the ribbon and top border at the same time, and you're ready to hang your quilt!

Assemble

1. Calculate how much ribbon you will need. To provide a 2" to 3" ribbon-folded casing, cut the ribbon to three times the length of the finished size of the quilt.

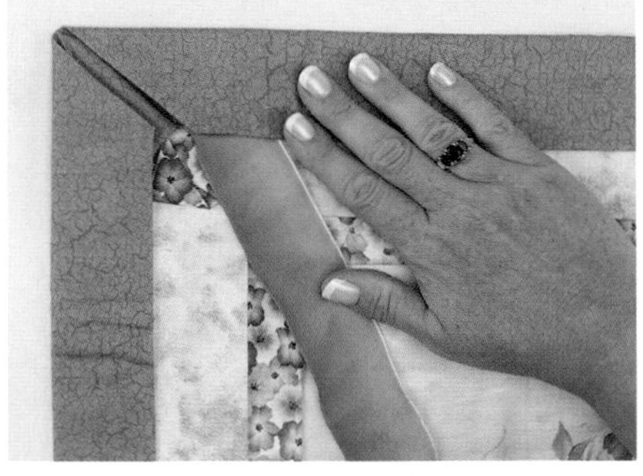

2. Slip one end of the ribbon beneath the still-unstitched edge of the top border. Hold or secure the ribbon in place, and pull it down at an angle.

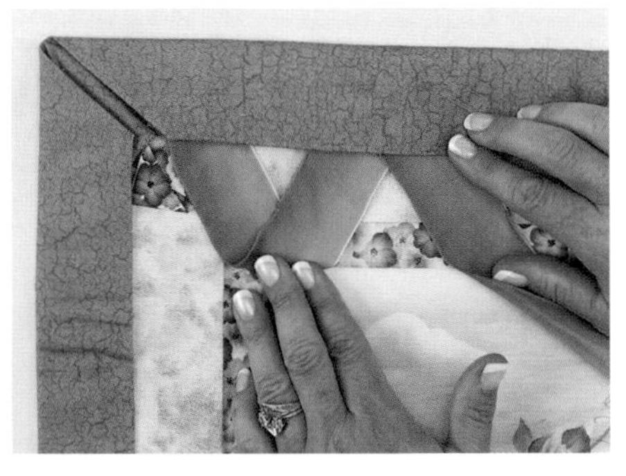

3. When the ribbon extends down 2" to 3", fold it back at an angle to the top border, and slip the fold under the edge of the border.

4. Continue to hold and fold the ribbon in a zigzag pattern across the width of the quilt. Work to keep the ribbon lengths consistent so the loops are a consistent size. To make defined folds, press the ribbon.

5. Sew the ribbon and top border in place. Flip the ribbon loops up, and hang the quilt as desired.

Quick-Turn Finish

The quick-turn finish often is used for purses, tote bags and simple projects, such as place mats or pillows.

Assemble

1. Cut the backing fabric 1" larger than the top of the project to be turned.

2. Place the backing fabric right sides together with the top of the quilt. Stitch with a ¼" seam allowance, leaving a 6" to 8" opening at the bottom of the project to turn the backing fabric right sides out.

3. Turn the project right side out. Press under the seam allowance of the opening from the right side of the fabric. Stitch the piece closed. Stitch ¼" inside the outside edge to form a faux binding.

Add-On Finish

The add-on finish method utilizes quick-turn, double-load strips of fabric to add borders to larger quilts. The corners on the final border can be straight or rounded.

Assemble

1. Cut a strip of fabric twice the finished width of the final border plus a ¼" seam allowance. Cut this strip crosswise if the length is less than 42"; otherwise cut the strip lengthwise.

2. Add fusible tape to the strip. Remove the paper tape from the strip.

3. Start pressing on the right side of the quick-turn, double-load strip from the front side of the quilt. Flip the border to the back side of the quilt. Remove the paper tape. Steam press the border to the quilt to hold it in place.

4. Press the border strips in the following order: top, bottom, side, side.

5. Stitch the finished border in place.

Rounded Corners

Assemble

1. Cut the ends of the top and bottom borders 2" longer than the quilt.

2. Use a small, rounded foam plate to trace a rounded corner on the wrong side of the strip. Stitch on the traced line, backstitching and stopping your stitching on the inside of the strip. Avoid catching the edge of the quilt when stitching.

3. Trim the corner within ⅛" of the stitching. Turn the border back to cover the unfinished edge of the quilt.

4. Use a dull pencil or seam turner to push the corners out.

Border-Fold Hanging Sleeve

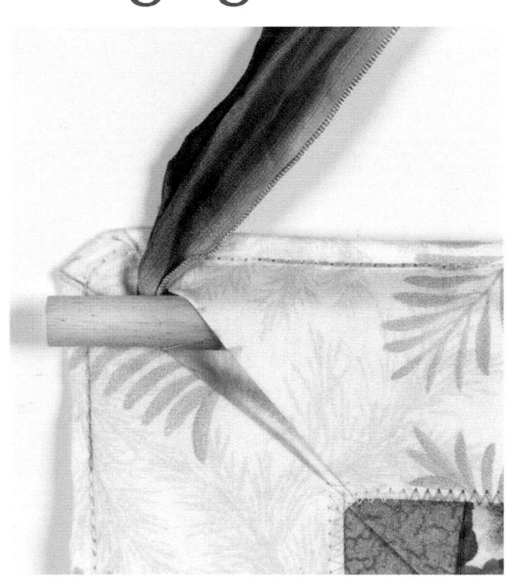

The border-fold hanging sleeve technique utilizes the backing fabric to form the final border and finished edge of your quilt. Because the corners of the border are not stitched down, you can slip a dowel rod through the border fold and use it to hang the quilt.

Assemble

1. Follow the step-by-step instructions for the double-fold border finish, except avoid stitching down the corners of the top border. Press each part of the fold as you go to ensure that the final border edge will lay flat for stitching, and press the corners flat to prevent them from opening.

2. Slip a dowel through the border. Attach ribbon to each end of the dowel. Hang as desired.

Projects, Patterns and Resources

Part 2

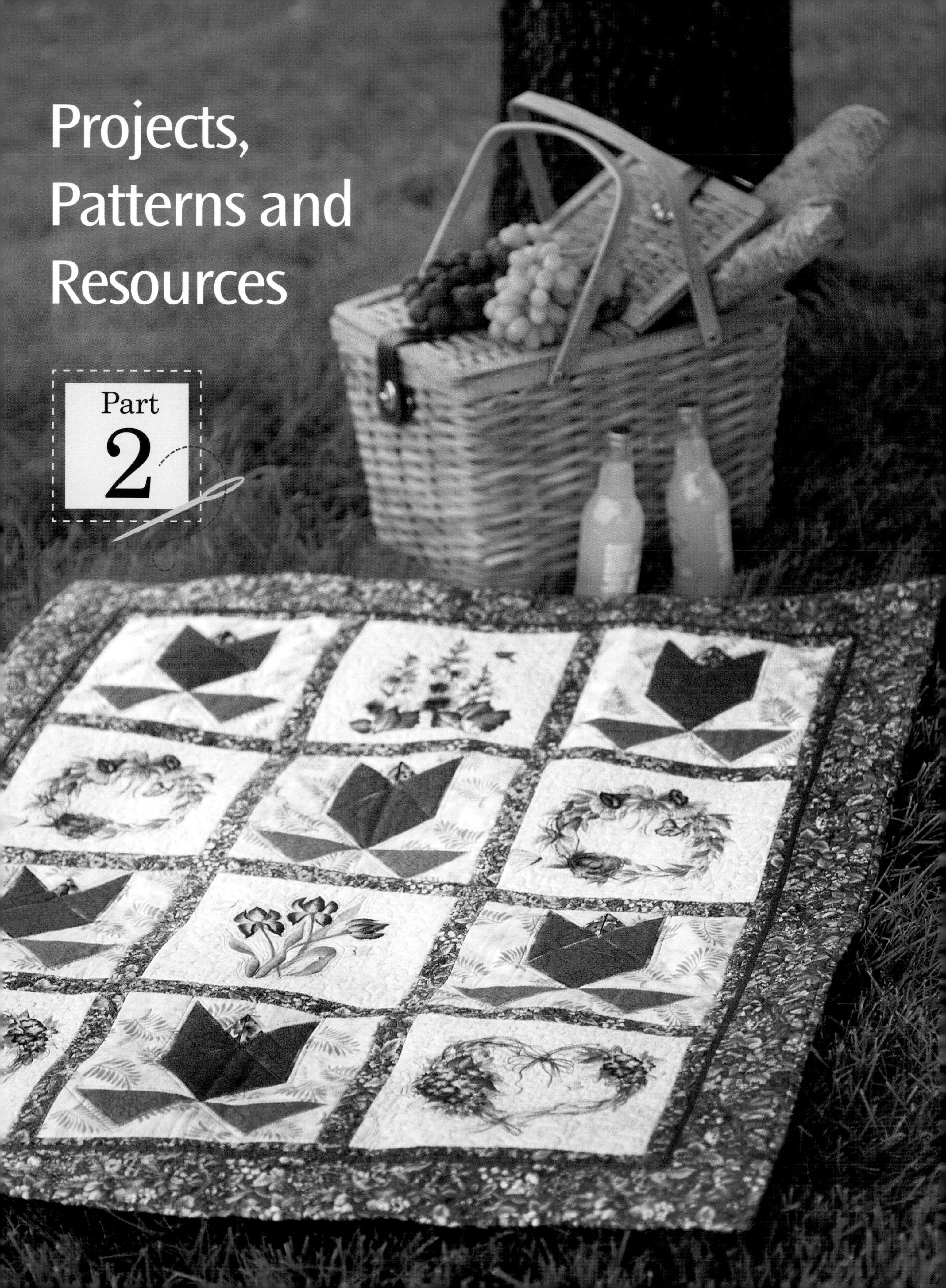

Garden Path Place Mats

Finished Size: 15" x 21"

These delightful place mats will take your table setting from ho-hum to fun. They boast a pair of triangles stitched into the binding that are perfect for holding silverware or pretty napkins.

Materials (For two place mats)

- ¼ yd. printed panel fabric or 2 Flower Pot Art to Sew blocks, each 10" square (center squares)
- 1½ yd. hunter green crackle or tonal print (backing, first border, fourth border)
- ⅝ yd. yellow fern print (second border)
- ⅛ yd. violet small floral (third border)
- Thread to complement the fabrics
- ½ yd. cotton batting
- 1 package fusible quilt top grid*
- Sewing tools and supplies

NOTE: One package of June Tailor Quilt Top Express is enough to make four Garden Path Place Mats and one Garden Path Table Runner

From	Cut	For
Printed panel/Art to Sew blocks	4 squares, 10" x 10"	Center squares
Hunter green crackle	2 strips, 2" x 42" 2 strips, 5" x 42" 2 rectangles, 16" x 22"	Single-fold strips for first border Single-fold strips for fourth border Backing
Yellow fern	4 strips, 5" x 42" 4 squares, 6" x 6"	Single-fold strips for second border Napkin fold corner finish
Violet floral	2 strips, 2" x 42"	Single-fold strips for third border
Batting	2 rectangles, 15" x 21"	Batting
Fusible quilt top grid	2 rectangles, 15" x 21"	Grid

Layer

1. Single-fold all of the strips wrong sides together. Press each strip in half.

2. Spray the batting with temporary spray adhesive. Place the grid, fusible side up, on top of the batting.

3. Place the center square on the grid.

Arrange

1. Place the first border strips on the top and bottom of the block; keep the folded edge against the raw edge. Cut the strips to fit.

2. Place one first border strip on each side of the block; keep the folded edge against the raw edge of the block. Cut the strips to fit.

3. Place one second border strip to each side of the block; keep the folded edges against the raw edge of the first border strips. Cut the strips to fit.

4. Add one second border strip to the top and bottom of the block; keep the folded edges against the raw edge of the first border strips.

5. Place a third border strip on each side of the block unit. Keep the folded edges against the raw edge of the first border strips. Cut the strips to fit.

6. Add the fourth border strip to the side edge of the block unit. Cut the strips to fit.

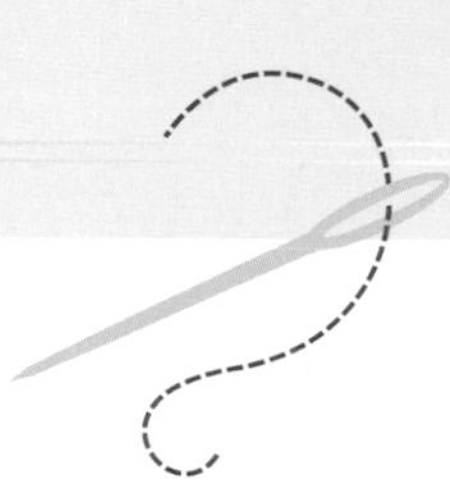

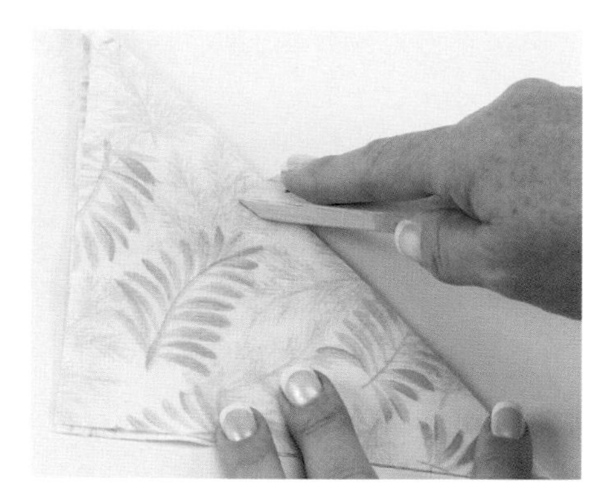

7. Fold and press two 6" squares in half on the diagonal to create two triangles.

8. Place one triangle on the left side of the place mat so it is against the bottom edge of the place mat and aligned with the raw edges of the second border. Place the second triangle in the mirror position on the right side of the place mat. Position the triangles so the third and fourth borders cover the raw edges.

9. Fold up the corners of the last border strip. Press a crease. Cut the corners on the crease line.

10. Press the strips and block to the fusible grid. You can use fabric glue or lightweight fusible tape to hold the fabric strips to the grid. Pin the center block through the fabric, grid and batting.

Stitch

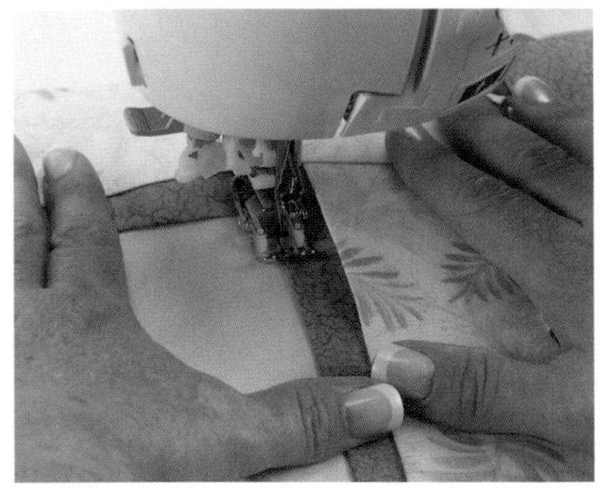

1. Use a zigzag, scallop or other decorative stitch to stitch around the center block, through all of the layers of fabric.

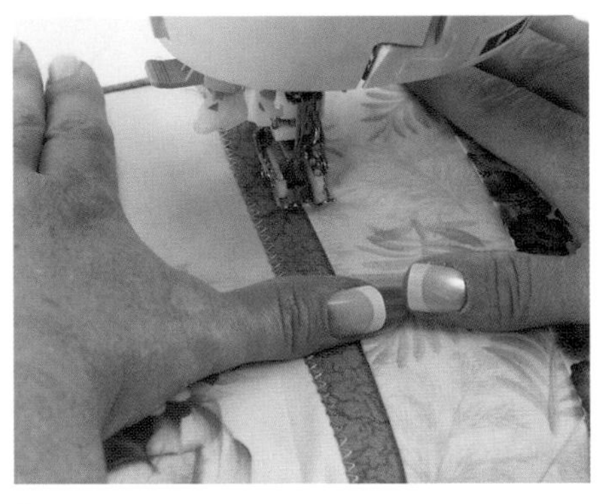

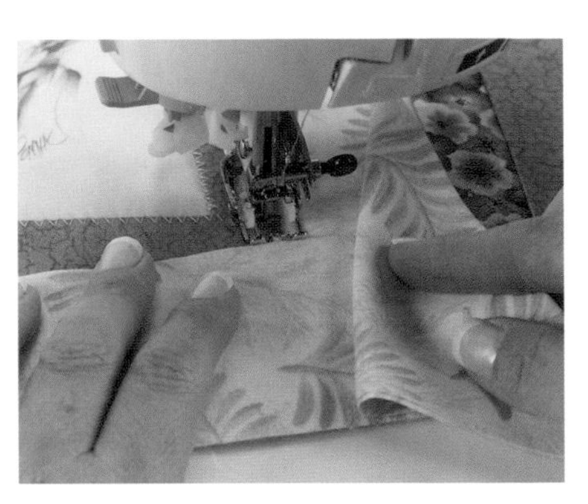

2. Stitch around the first border. Move each of the side triangles to avoid stitching the long edges down.

3. Stitch around the second border; be sure to stitch down the side edges of each triangle.

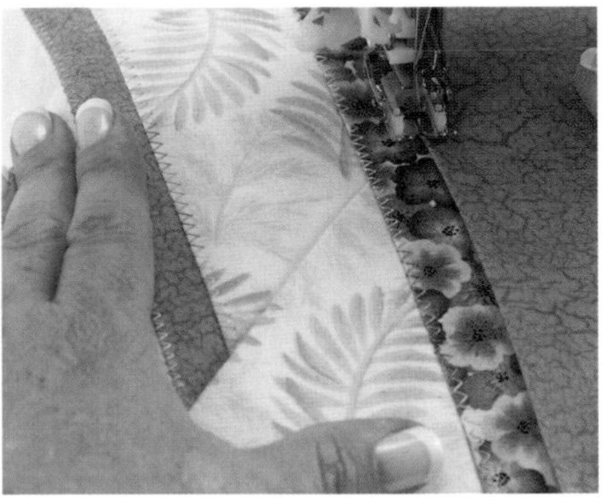

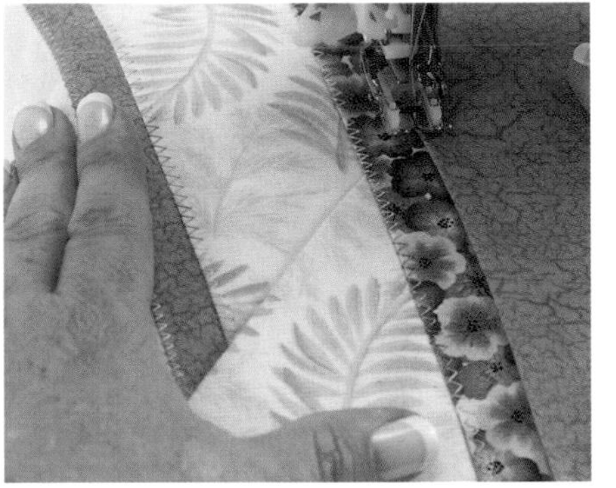

4. Stitch around the third and fourth borders. Trim any extra batting or grid so the layers are even with the fabric.

5. Place the backing fabric right sides together with the top of the place mat. Stitch with a ¼" seam allowance, leaving a 6" opening at the bottom of the place mat to turn the backing fabric right side out.

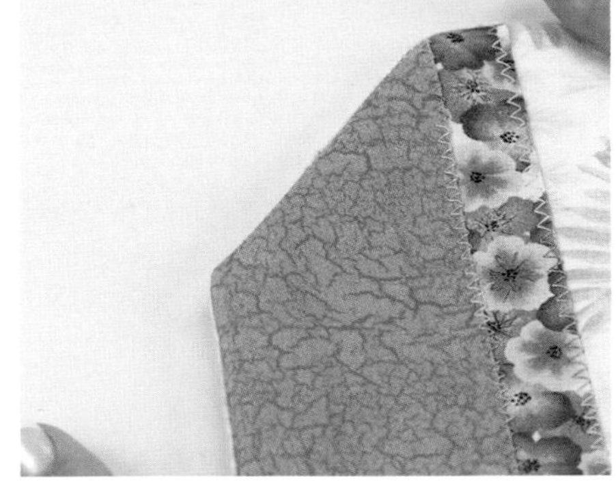

6. Turn the place mat right side out. Press under the raw edge, then stitch the opening closed. Stitch ¼" inside the outside edge to form a faux binding.

Tip

Use variegated decorative thread to enhance the appearance of the finished project.

Variation: Tulip Patch Place Mats

Finished Size: 15" x 21"

Make a set of patchwork-themed place mats that are guaranteed to please. Follow the same instructions for the Garden Path Place Mats, except adjust your fabric needs to create a patchwork block of your choosing, such as the tulip block, from the One Stitch Block Gallery. Complete your table setting by slipping a coordinating napkin in one of the triangle corners.

Garden Path Napkins

Finished Size: 16½" x 16½" x 23½" triangle

Add pizazz to your table setting with quick and easy cloth napkins. Their triangular shape makes these napkins perfect to tuck into coordinating Garden Path Place Mats.

Materials

(For two napkins)

- ⅝ yd. violet small floral print
- Thread to complement the fabric
- Sewing tools and supplies

From	Cut	For
Violet floral	2 squares, 18" x 18"	2 napkins

Layer and Arrange

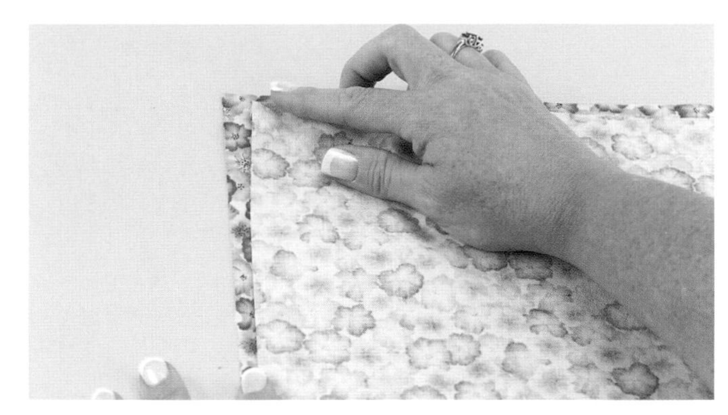

1. Fold each 18" square in half on the diagonal, right sides together.

Stitch

1. Sew ¼" around the raw edges, leaving roughly 5" open on one side of the napkin.

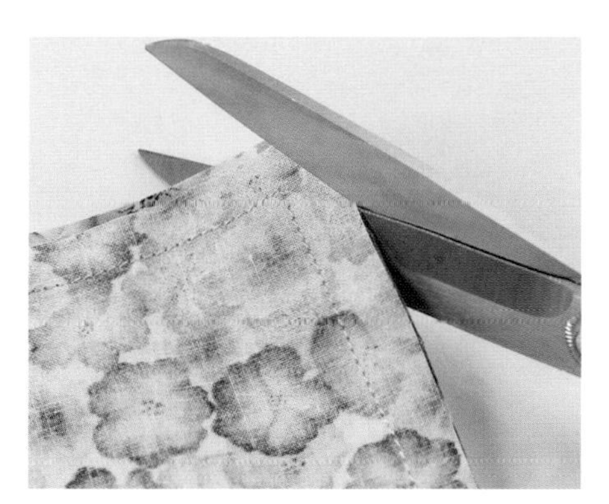

2. Clip the corners so the napkin is easier to turn.

3. Turn the napkin right side out. Use a bamboo stiletto or the end of a seam ripper to push the corners out.

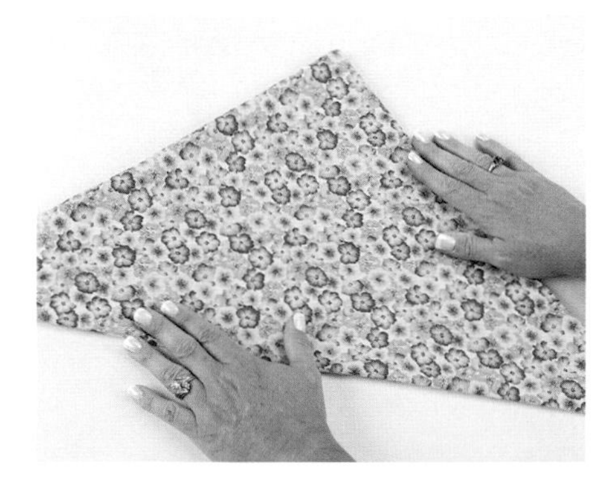

4. Press the napkin flat.

5. Topstitch ¼" around the outside edge of the napkin.

Garden Path Table Runner

Finished Size: 16" x 36"

Whether it serves as a backdrop for candles and fresh flowers or your family's favorite casserole, the Garden Path Table Runner adds a decorator touch to your dining room table. It's so easy, you can start the runner after lunch and finish it in time for supper.

Materials

- 3 Garden Path Art to Sew or other printed blocks of your choice, or enough fabric to create 3 One Stitch blocks of your choice (center square)
- 1 yd. violet small floral print (backing, first border)
- ½ yd. hunter green crackle or tonal print (sashing)
- ½ yd. yellow fern print (second border)
- Thread to complement the project
- Batting
- Fusible quilt grid
- Sewing tools and supplies

From	Cut	For
Hunter green crackle	2 strips, 2½" x 42" 1 strip, 3" x 42"	Single-fold strip for sashing Double-fold strip for sashing
Yellow fern	3 strips, 5" x 42"	Single-fold strips for second border
Violet floral	6 strips, 2½" x 42" 1 rectangle, 18" x 38"	Single-fold strips for first border, quick-turn strips Backing
Printed/Art to Sew blocks	3 blocks, 10" x 10"	Center squares
Quilt grid	1 rectangle, 16" x 36"	Quilt grid
Batting	1 rectangle, 16" x 36"	Batting

Layer

1. Fold each strip wrong sides together. Press each strip in half to create a single-fold strip.

2. Open out the fold on the 3" strip. Refold both raw edges toward the crease line in the middle of the strip; press to yield two folded edges, which form a double-fold strip.

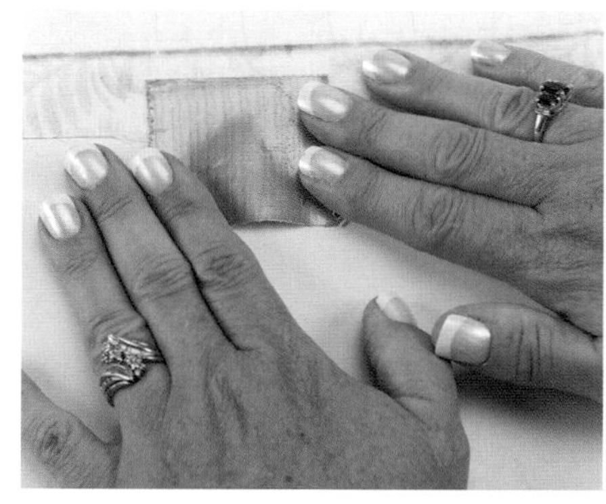

3. Use 2"-wide duct tape or masking tape to anchor the backing fabric wrong side up to the table.

4. Center the quilt grid on top of the batting, fusible side down. Set your iron to a medium heat setting, then lightly press the grid to the batting. Center the batting/grid sandwich in the center of the backing fabric. An even amount of backing should show around the top of the quilt.

Arrange

1. Mark an X on the center of the grid. Spray the grid surface with temporary spray adhesive.

Tip

Experiment with different finishing styles for your projects. The table runner can as easily be finished using quick-turn strips as it can by creating a faux border from the backing.

2. Fold each center square in quarters, and finger crease the folds. Place the first center block on the grid; match the center crease of the block with the X on the grid.

◀ 3. Place the second and third center squares on either side of the first center square; be sure to position each center square so its edge matches the one next to it.

4. Cut one strip, 10" long, from each 2½"-wide single-fold hunter green crackle strip. Cut two strips, each 10" long, from the 3"-wide double-fold hunter green crackle strip.

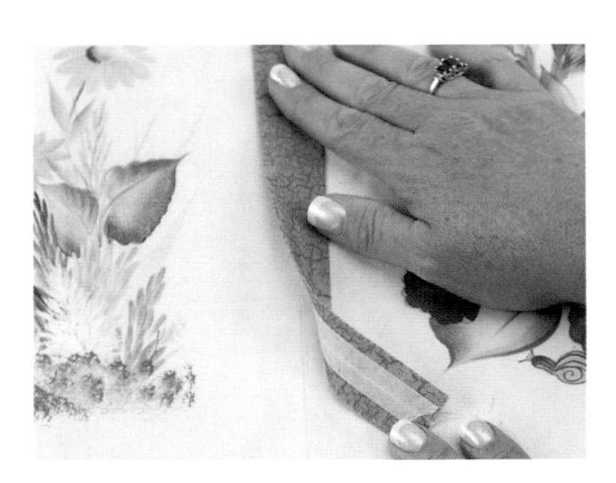

5. Place the two wider 10"-long strips between the blocks. Place the two narrower 10"-long strips on each end of the blocks.

6. Place one long, single-fold sashing strip above the center squares and another below; keep the folded side against the raw edge of the block.

7. Trim the length of the strips to fit.

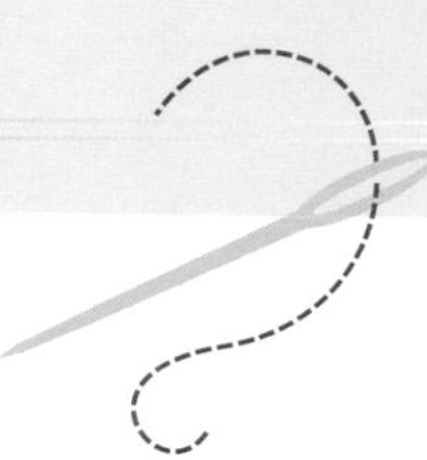

8. Place the first border strips on the short sides of the center squares; keep the folded edges against the raw edges of the sashing strips. Add the long strips. Cut the strips to fit.

9. Repeat Step 8 with the second border strips, starting with the short sides first, and then covering the long sides of the quilt top.

10. Press the strips and blocks to the fusible quilt grid. If needed, use fabric glue to hold everything in place, or insert lightweight fusible tape between the grid and strips to hold pieces in place. If desired, use safety pins to pin through all of the layers to secure the blocks and strips.

Stitch

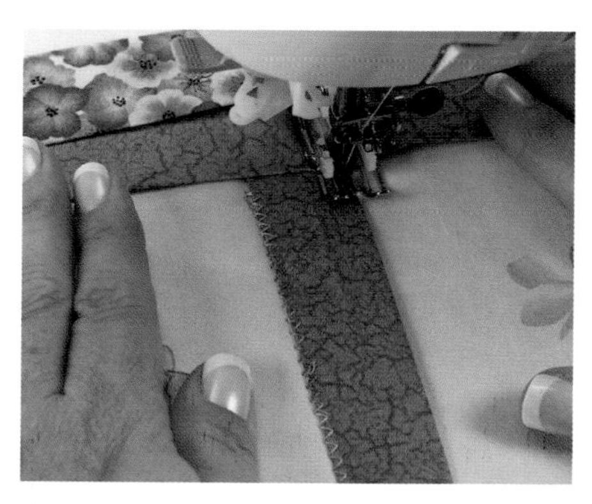

1. Replace your sewing machine's presser foot with a walking foot. Zigzag stitch around the sashing around the middle block of the quilt top. Continue to stitch all of the short sashing strips, then stitch the long sashing strips.

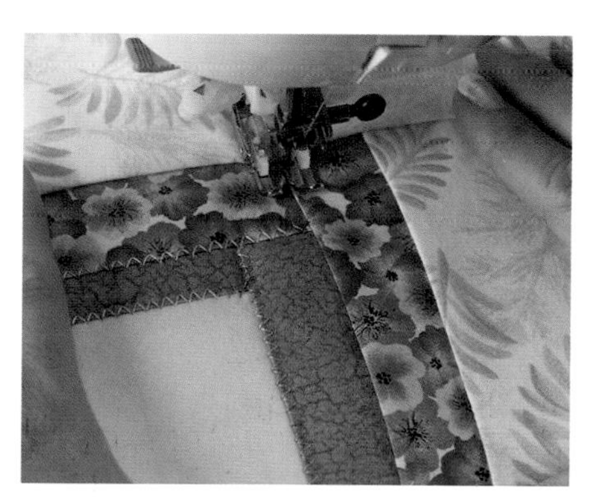

2. Stitch the first border.

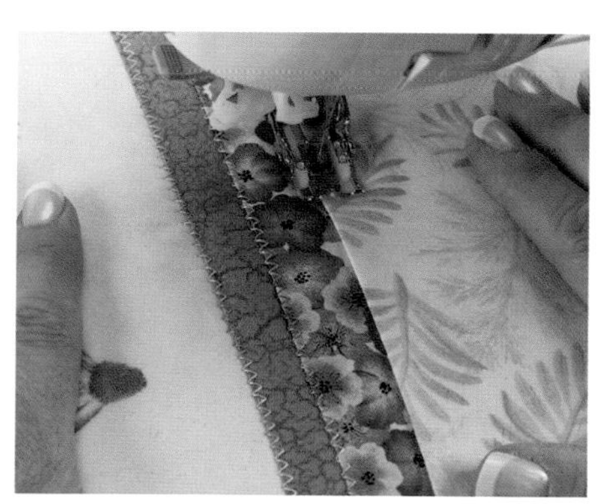

3. Stitch the second border.

4. Press the quilt sandwich. Trim the layers so they are even.

5. Create the quick-turn strips. Single-fold four 2½"-wide violet floral strips in half lengthwise, placing the fabric wrong sides together. Open each strip. Press ½" fusible tape on the long edge on the right side of the fabric of each side of each strip. Leave the paper in place. Using the paper-backed tape as your guide, turn under a ½" seam allowance to the wrong side. Press the tape under.

6. Pull the paper tape off of a quick-turn strip. Overlap ½" of the edge of the quick-turn fold strip over the long sides of the runner.

7. Steam press the strip to hold it in place. Stitch the quick-turn strip to the edge of the runner.

8. Cut the strip to fit.

9. Repeat Steps 6 through 8 on the opposite edge of the quilt.

10. For the sides of the quilt, press the quick-turn strips in place up to 6" from each corner. Allow the ends of the strip to extend 2" past the edge of the runner. Leave the ends open; turn the edges right sides together to finish the corner.

11. Press the quilt's edges in place. Use a zigzag stitch to sew along the inside edge of the border and secure the finish.

Variation: Picture Perfect Runner

Finished Size: 16" x 36"

Display your treasured photos with the Picture Perfect Runner. Follow the same general instructions for the Garden Path Table Runner, except use fabric prints of your favorite photos instead of preprinted fabric blocks or patchwork squares, and adjust your materials list accordingly. See the One Stitch Block Gallery for detailed instructions.

When you add the photo blocks, you can either fuse the entire photo square as it is printed, or you can cut out a specific element of the photo and fuse it to a complementary-colored background square.

After you begin stitching, go back to each center square. Quilt around the key motifs of each photo. If you cut out a specific element of a photo, try adding free-motion quilting to the background square to add visual interest.

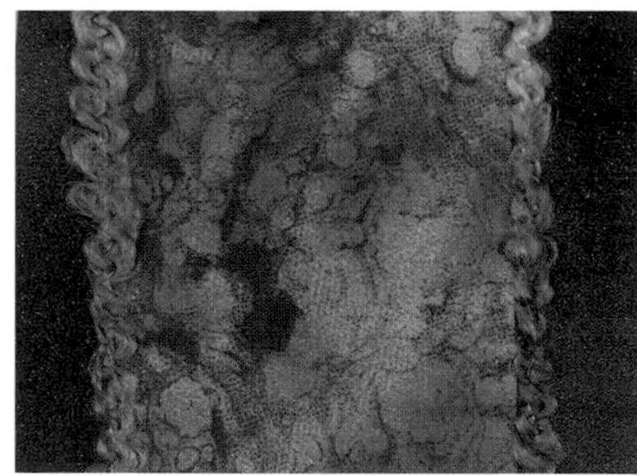

If desired, embellish the runner with fuzzy yarn or another trim of your choosing. Use a zigzag stitch to secure the trim around the blocks and borders of the quilt.

Jacob's Star Wall Quilt

Finished Size: 38" x 38"

The classic elements of the Jacob's Ladder and Ohio Star blocks combine to create this new look: The Jacob's Star Wall Quilt. Easy-to-make envelope roses add a dimensional accent to dress up this quilt.

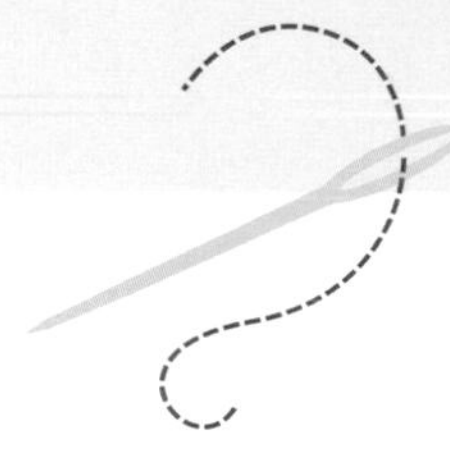

Materials 

- 1¼ yd. pink, orange and gold large-scale floral print (center square, blocks, border)
- 1 yd. green sponge or batik (background)
- ¾ yd. hunter green crackle or tonal print (accent 1)
- ¾ yd. grass green crackle or tonal print (accent 2)
- 1 yd. green fern print (backing)
- 1¼ yd. fusible web interfacing
- 8 yd. fusible tape, ½" wide
- 2 yd. needled cotton batting
- 1 package fusible grid
- Sewing tools and supplies

From	Cut	For
Large-scale floral	1 strip, 4½" x 45"; cut again into 8 squares, 4½" x 4½" 4 strips, 9" x 45"; from 2 of the strips, cut 2 squares, 9" x 9" 4 squares, 2" x 2"	Squares Outside border Envelope rose buds
Green sponge	1 square, 29" x 29"	Background
Hunter green crackle	1 strip, 4½" x 45"; cut again to yield 4 squares, 4½" x 4½" 2 squares, 2" x 2"; cut each square once on the diagonal to yield 4 triangles	Squares Envelope rose leaves
Grass green crackle	1 square, 9" x 9"; cut again twice on the diagonal to yield 4 triangles 4 strips, 2" x 42"	Triangles for star Inner border
Green fern	1 square, 34" x 34"	Backing
Batting	4 strips, 3½" x 45" 4 strips, 3" x 45" 1 square, 33" x 33"	Strips Strips Main quilt top batting
Fusible quilt grid	1 square, 33" x 33"	Main quilt top grid

Layer

1. Use a dry iron on a medium setting to fuse the quilt grid to the batting.

2. Cut the grid/batting sandwich to a 31" x 31" square.

3. Lay the backing fabric wrong side up. Spray the wrong side of the backing fabric with temporary spray adhesive to make it tacky.

4. Fold the grid/batting sandwich in half, and position it grid side up on the backing fabric. Smooth down the grid/batting, and secure it to the backing fabric.

5. Spray the top of the grid/batting with temporary spray adhesive to make it tacky. Place the 29" x 29" background square right side up on top of the grid so 1" of grid/batting is visible around all four sides of the background. Lightly hand press the background square in place.

6. Place all of the square and triangle patches onto the sticky side of the fusible web. Use a steam iron to press the patches on the paper side of the web. Cut out the patches, but leave the paper backing in place until you lay out your quilt design on the backing fabric.

Arrange

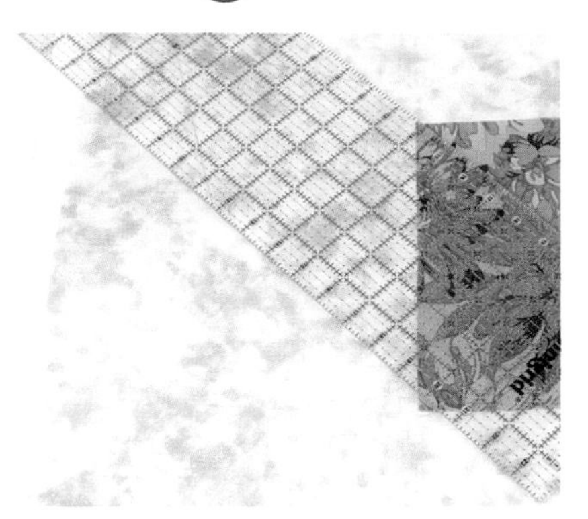

1. Fold the 9" large-scale floral square into quarters; hand crease the folds. Unfold the square and place it right side up on top of the background fabric, centering it on all four sides. Each outside edge of center square should be 10" from the outside edge of the background square.

2. Place the long edge of a large triangle right side up against one outside edge of the center square. Repeat for the remaining large triangles. Remove the paper backing, and lightly hand press the triangles in place.

3. Working from the center of the quilt out, place the eight 4½" squares of the large-scale fabric right side up onto the top of the background fabric. Once you are happy with the arrangement, pull the paper backing off the squares and lightly hand press the pieces to the quilt.

4. Add the final triangle patches to the quilt top to complete the star pattern as shown.

5. Remove the paper backing from the triangle pieces and lightly hand press them in place. Step back, survey the quilt and ensure that all of the pieces are aligned from the center out. There should be a 1" margin of background fabric all around the quilt, which will allow you to add the borders without clipping the points of the star. Adjust any pieces as needed, then use a steam iron to press the patches into place.

6. Fold the 2" border strips in half, wrong sides together, and press the strips. Press one strip of ½" fusible tape down the center of each border strip. Remove the paper backing from the strip.

7. Place the folded edge of the top border strip against the edges of the patches; make sure each strip covers the 1" margin of background. Trim the ends of each strip even with the edge of the background square.

8. Add the bottom border strip; trim the ends even with the background edge. Press it in place. Add the side border strips; overlap the top and bottom border strips. Trim the ends even with the edge of the background.

Stitch

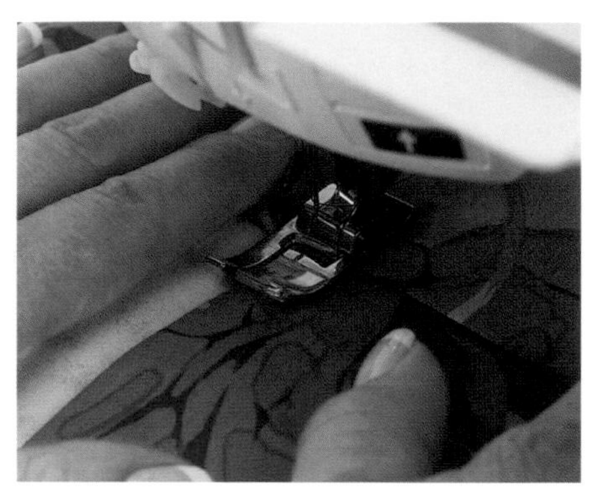

◀ 1. Stitch through all of the patches as shown. Sew the vertical lines first, the horizontal lines second and the diagonal lines of the triangle third. Stitch down the folded edge of the borders, ¼" from the outside edge of the quilt. Trim off the excess grid/batting.

2. Press a strip of ½" fusible tape to the right side of the long side of each 9" border strip. Each strip of fusible tape should be against the edge of the fabric. Leave the tape and backing in place. Flip each strip over. Use the tape as a guide to fold over a ½" seam allowance. Press each folded edge flat. Fold each strip in half, wrong sides together, and press.

3. Open each border strip. Load a 3½" strip of batting inside each border strip. Make sure the batting is tucked under the turned fabric edge. Load a 3" strip of batting on top of the first batting layer in each strip.

◀ 4. Remove the paper backing from the fusible tape on each of the 9" border strips. Add a 9" border strip to the top edge of the quilt. Steam press the strip from the top of the quilt to hold it in place. Flip the quilt over; steam press the strip from the back of the quilt to firmly attach the strip. Trim the edges of the strip even with the quilt edges.

5. Repeat Step 4 to add a border strip to the bottom edge of the quilt.

6. Slip the edge of the double-load strip over the side edge of the quilt and over the edge of the top and bottom border. Steam press the strip about 10" from the middle of the quilt to hold it in place; avoid pressing the edges of the side strip down.

7. Flip the top of the border over onto itself, right sides together. Slip the top edge about ⅛" beyond the back of the border to ensure that the border covers the top edge of the quilt. Starting ½" inside the outside edge, stitch the seam; backstitch to the outside edge, and then stitch up to the outside edge to form a closed corner seam. Trim the seam allowance to ½". Clip the corners. Repeat for the other end of the side strip.

8. Repeat Steps 6 and 7 for the second side strip.

9. Turn the strip right side out; bring it back to the front of the quilt. Smooth it in place; make sure the corner is neatly turned down. Press the strip in place. Use a zigzag stitch to sew the strip in place from the top side of the quilt; be sure to catch both sides of the strip with the stitches.

Stars in My Garden Wall Hanging

Finished Size: 27" x 27"

Sparkling yarn trim, an appliquéd center block and striking fabrics transform an otherwise simple Four-Patch Variation block into a piece of art. Try experimenting with trims and fabrics to achieve different looks.

Materials

- ⅝ yd. cream crackle or tonal print (star block background square)
- ¼ yd. black or other solid color to match background of large-scale floral (center square)
- 2 yd. large-scale pink, purple, orange, green and gold floral with black background (cutouts, star and backing/third border)
- 1 yd. dark green print (star, second border)
- ⅓ yd. hot pink batik (star, first border)
- Fusible web
- Coordinating thread
- 1 package fusible quilt grid
- 1 yd. cotton batting
- Fusible tape in ½" and ⅝" widths
- 1 skein fuzzy yarn, optional
- Sewing tools and supplies

From	Cut	For
Hot pink batik	3 strips, 2" x 42" 2 squares, 4½" x 4½"	Single-fold strips for first border Star patches
Dark green print	4 strips, 5" x 42" 4 squares, 3⅛" x 3⅛"	Single-fold strips for second border Star patches
Large-scale floral	2 squares, 4½" x 4½" 1 square, 42½" x 42½" Floral motifs (fussy cut)	Star patches Backing/border fabric Appliqué cutouts in center square
Cream crackle	1 square, 20" x 20"	Patchwork block background
Black solid	1 square, 9" x 9"	Background for center square
Batting	1 square 30" x 30"	Batting
Fusible quilt grid	1 square, 30" x 30"	Quilt top grid

Layer

1. Place all of the 3⅛" squares and 4½" squares on fusible web. Fuse the patches.

2. Use a dry iron on a medium setting to fuse the grid to the batting.

3. Fold the backing fabric in half vertically, then horizontally. Press the creases.

4. Lay out the backing fabric wrong side up. Spray the wrong side of the backing fabric with temporary spray adhesive to make it tacky.

5. Fold the grid/batting sandwich in half. Place it grid side up onto the backing fabric; the fabric should be even on each side of the batting. Smooth the grid/batting sandwich in place, and secure it to the backing fabric. Spray the grid with temporary spray adhesive.

6. Appliqué the fussy-cut floral pieces to the black center square. For information, see the One Stitch Block Gallery in Part 1.

Arrange

1. Fold the 20" square of background fabric in half on the diagonal. Press the crease. Repeat for the opposite diagonal.

2. Lay the 20" square of background fabric right side up on top of the grid. Lightly hand press the square in place; 5" of grid should show on each side of the background square.

3. Place the 9" appliquéd center square right side up on top of the background fabric; align each corner with a diagonal crease line of the background square to ensure the block is centered.

4. Begin laying out the patches for the star by positioning two pink triangles on each side of the center square as shown; be sure to butt the long side of each pink triangle up against the corresponding outside edge of the center square so no background fabric shows through. Remove the paper backing, and lightly hand press each patch in place.

5. Position each large-scale floral triangle so each floral triangle's short side is butted against the short side of each pink triangle. Remove the paper backing, and lightly hand press each patch in place.

6. Add the green square patches; position each patch between two triangles so one point touches the center square. Remove the paper backing, and lightly hand press each patch in place.

7. Step back and survey your wall hanging. Make sure that all of the pieces are aligned from the center out and a 1" margin of background fabric is visible all the way around the star. Use a steam iron to press all of the patches in place.

8. Press one strip of ½" fusible tape down the center of each pink border strip to create a single-fold strip. See Part 1 for detailed instructions. Remove the backing paper.

9. Starting at the top of the quilt, place the folded edge of the strip against the edges of the patches so the pink strip covers up the 1" margin of background. Trim the strip's ends even with the background's edge. Press the strip in place.

10. Repeat Step 9 to add the bottom pink border strip. Press the strip in place.

11. Add the side border strips; make sure the side strips overlap the top and bottom strips. Trim the ends of the side strips so they are even with the edge of the background.

12. Press one strip of ½"-wide fusible tape down the center of each green strip. Remove the paper backing.

13. Starting at the top of the wall hanging, place the folded side of the strip so it overlaps ¼" inside the raw edge of the first border. Extend the ends of the strip to the edge of the grid at the 24" line. Cut the strip even with the 24" grid line. Repeat for the bottom strip.

14. Place the folded side of another green strip toward the right side of the wall hanging; overlap the raw edges of the first border. Extend the ends of the strip across the top and bottom border strips. Repeat for the left strip.

15. Cut each side strip so the outside edges are even with the outside edges of the top and bottom borders.

16. Fold under a corner of the right and left borders at each end of the wall hanging. Press the folded corner to create a mitered border. Place a strip of ⅝"-wide fusible tape under the miter fold. Press the fold to hold the fabric in place.

17. Fold each corner of the backing fabric up to the edge of the batting to form a triangle. Press the crease.

18. Fold the four sides of the backing fabric once toward the batting. Place the raw edge even with the batting. Press.

19. Cut a square from the tip of each floral fabric triangle so the resulting notch reveals the corner where the green strips meet.

20. Fold the backing fabric in half again, this time so the folded edge of the floral fabric overlaps the edge of the green border. Place a strip of ⅝"-wide fusible tape under the miter fold; press the fold to hold the fabric in place.

Stitch

1. Use safety pins to pin through all of the layers of the quilt; avoid pinning across seams.

2. Replace the sewing machine's presser foot with a walking foot. Starting with the cutouts in the center square, use a feather, zigzag or other decorative stitch with a width of no more than 3.5 and a length of 2.5 to stitch through all of the layers of the quilt and outline the motifs as shown.

3. Continue to stitch out from the center. Stitch down the long sides of the first border first, then turn the wall hanging around to stitch on the other long side. Stitch down the final border around all of the outside edges. If desired, leave the corners at the top open for a hanging sleeve.

4. If desired, accent the quilt with a yarn embellishment. For the wall hanging shown, yarn was stitched around the outside edges of the center square and between the second and outside borders.

Pansy Wreath Pillow

Finished Size: 18" x 18"

Whip up a pile of these pillows to give your favorite room a face-lift. This project has an added bonus: Hook and loop tape closures make it a breeze to remove the pillow cover for laundering. This project easily converts to a wall hanging; just skip the steps to add the pillow back. See the variations for three very different approaches to the same project.

Materials

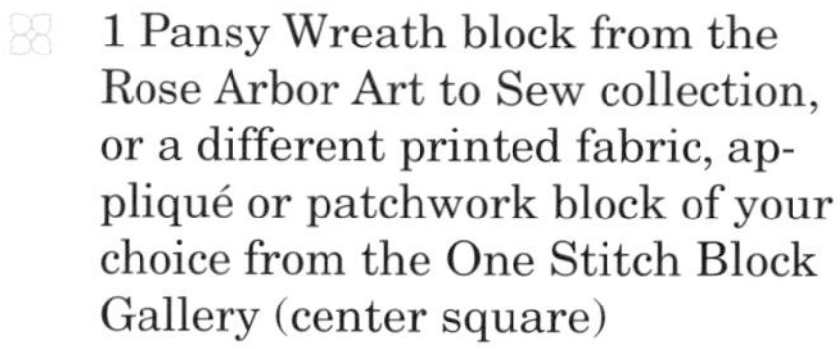

- 1 Pansy Wreath block from the Rose Arbor Art to Sew collection, or a different printed fabric, appliqué or patchwork block of your choice from the One Stitch Block Gallery (center square)
- 1 purple crackle or tonal print fat quarter (first border)
- 1 violet sponge or batik print fat quarter (second border)
- 1½ yd. green fern print (pillow back, third border/backing fabric)
- ⅛ yd. violet small floral print (folded roses)
- Green thread to match the third border
- 1 package fusible quilt top grid
- ½ yd. cotton batting
- 14" x 14" pillow form
- ⅓ yd. hook and loop tape, ½" to ¾" wide
- Sewing tools and supplies

From	Cut	For
Art to Sew block/other fabric	1 square, 10" x 10"	Center square
Purple crackle	2 strips, 2½" x 22"	Single-fold strips, first border
Violet sponge	2 strips, 4½" x 22"	Single-fold strips, second border
Green fern	1 square, 26" x 26" 2 rectangles, 9" x 16"	Backing/last border Pillowback
Violet floral	4 squares, 2½" x 2½"	Folded roses
Quilt top grid	1 square, 18" x 18"	Quilt top grid
Batting	1 square, 18" x 18"	Batting

Layer

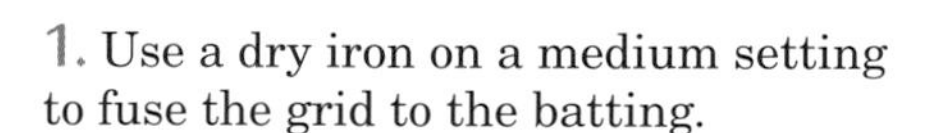

1. Use a dry iron on a medium setting to fuse the grid to the batting.

2. Fold the backing fabric in half vertically, then horizontally. Press the creases.

3. Lay out the backing fabric wrong side up. Spray the wrong side of the backing fabric with temporary spray adhesive to make it tacky.

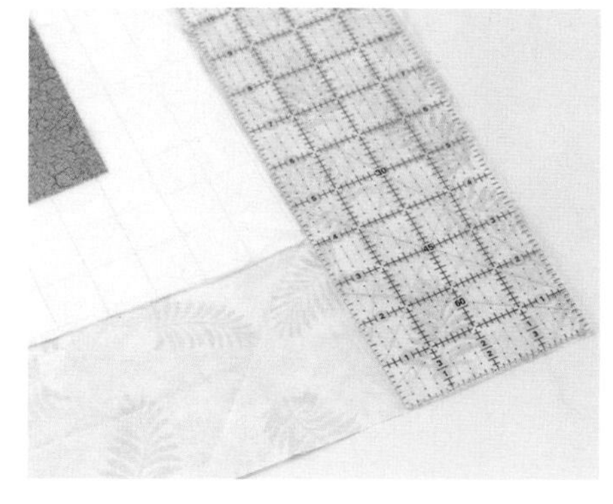

◀ 4. Fold the grid/batting sandwich in half. Center it grid side up on the backing fabric so 4" of backing fabric is visible on each side of the batting as shown. Smooth the grid/batting sandwich in place, and secure it to the backing fabric. Spray the grid with temporary spray adhesive.

5. Create single-fold strips from the purple crackle and violet floral for the first and second borders. For detailed instructions, refer to One Stitch Strips in Part 1.

Arrange

1. Fold the center square in half to find its center. Count the squares on your grid, and match the center of the block to the center of the grid. Smooth the block into place; if needed, pin the block to keep it in position.

2. Place a first border single-fold strip on each side of the center square; line up the raw edges of the strip with the first grid line outside of the center square. The folded edge of the strip should overlap the raw edge of the block on both sides by ¼". Repeat to add a single-fold strip to the top and bottom of the block. If desired, pin through the layers to secure the strips.

3. Repeat the process from Step 2 for the second border strips. If desired, pin through the layers to secure the strips.

4. Fold each corner of the backing fabric toward the batting to create a triangle whose point touches the corner of the batting. Press each corner in place.

5. Fold each corner of the backing fabric again. The folded edge from the corner will overlap the purple sponge print border at the corner. Press.

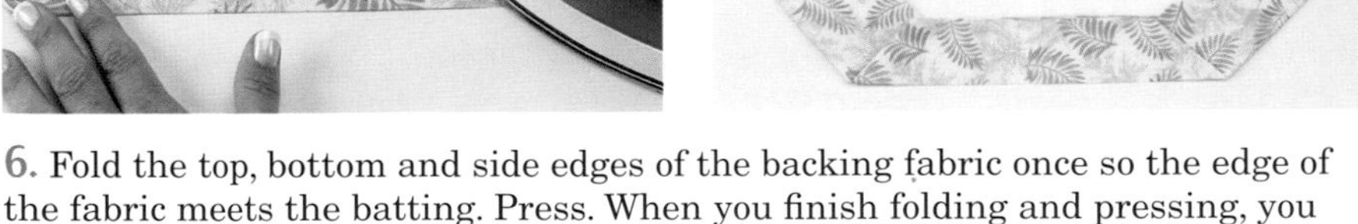

6. Fold the top, bottom and side edges of the backing fabric once so the edge of the fabric meets the batting. Press. When you finish folding and pressing, you will have an octagon-shaped piece.

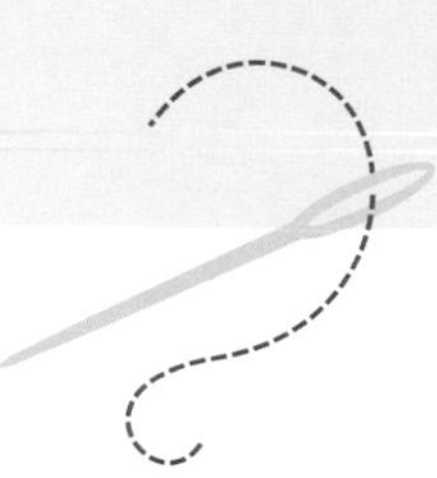

7. Fold the top and bottom edges of the backing fabric again toward the center of the quilt. Repeat for the sides of the quilt to create mitered corners. If desired, use fabric glue to secure the corners.

8. Add folded roses at each corner, just inside the final border. For detailed instructions, see One Stitch Embellishments in Part 1.

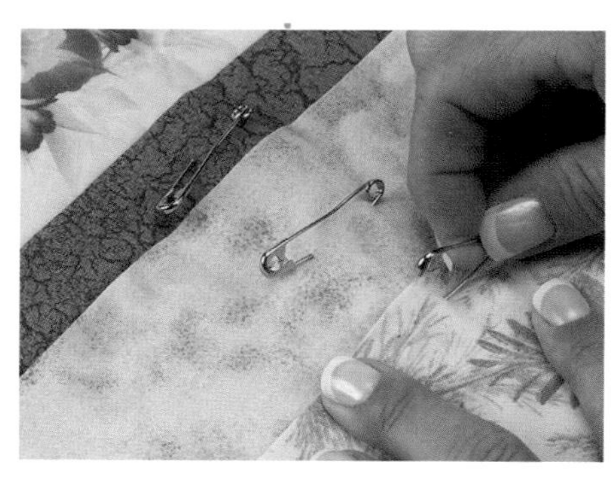

9. Use No. 2 safety pins to pin all of the layers in preparation for stitching.

Stitch

1. Replace the presser foot on your sewing machine with a walking foot. Starting with the first border, use a straight or narrow zigzag stitch to stitch through all of the layers.

2. Continue stitching until you have secured all of the borders and envelope roses.

3. Use the two 9" x 16" fabric panels and hook and loop tape to add the pillow back finish. For detailed instructions, refer to One Stitch Finishes in Part 1.

4. Insert the pillow form.

Variation: Chasing Butterflies Wall Hanging

Finished Size: 18" x 18"

Bring a touch of summer into your home with the Chasing Butterflies Wall Hanging. The fun, colorful backing fabric is the perfect partner for the butterfly patchwork block.

Refer to the One Stitch Block Gallery for specific materials and instructions to make the butterfly block. Follow the same instructions as for the Pansy Pillow, except skip the steps for the pillow back detail. You may wish to alter your stitching along the top border to create a built-in hanging sleeve.

Add a realistic finishing touch to the butterfly block by freehand-stitching a pair of antennae.

Variation: Morning Bouquet Miniature Quilt

Finished Size: 18" x 18"

Here's a new way to showcase a treasured piece of needlework.

Follow the same general instructions for the Pansy Wreath Pillow and Chasing Butterflies Wall Hanging, except replace the patchwork center square with a completed piece of needlework; a cross-stitched piece was used for this project. Before you cut the needlework, fold its edges to make sure it fits well within in the space planned.

Be sure to use a neutral background fabric so the stitching shines through — not the fabric pattern.

Adjust the border strip sizes as needed around the stitched motif to frame the piece to its best advantage. In this piece, the cross-stitched center piece measures 6¼" x 7". The borders vary slightly in width and length; the outside edges of the finished second border measure 10½" x 10½".

If you have several pieces of needlework, make a cozy nest of coordinating pillows; just follow the instructions in the Pansy Wreath Pillow project.

Rose Arbor Wall Quilt

Finished Size: 28" x 28"

Replace that artwork you've grown tired of without digging out your paints or making a trip to the framing gallery — just plan a little time in your sewing room! Search the variety of printed panels available on the market to find the right fabric to fit your space and mood.

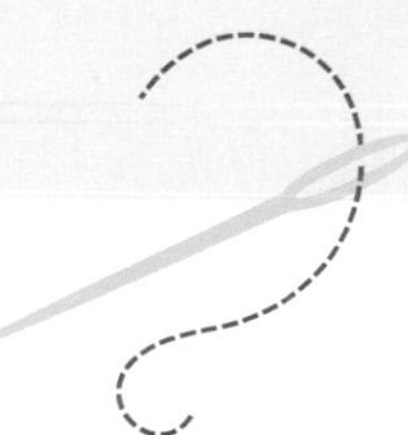

Tip

Different choices in fabrics, embellishments, finish treatments and border numbers and widths can make a huge difference in the way the finished wall quilt looks. Experiment with your choices to create a custom piece of art worthy of a spot above your mantel.

Materials

- 1 large Rose Arbor block from the Rose Arbor Art to Sew collection, or another large scale appliqué, printed panel, patchwork or novelty block of your choice
- ¼ yd. dark-colored small floral print (first border)
- ⅝ yd. light-colored tonal print (second border)
- 1 yd. dark-colored tonal print (third border, backing)
- ⅛ yd. medium-colored small floral print (envelope roses)
- Thread to match the third border
- 1 package fusible quilt top grid
- 1 yd. cotton batting
- Sewing tools and supplies

From	Cut	For
Printed panel block	1 square, 18" x 18"	Center square
Dark floral	2 strips, 2" x 42"	Single-fold strips/first border
Light tonal	4 strips, 5" x 42"	Single-fold strips/second border
Medium floral	4 squares, 2½" x 2½"	Envelope roses
Dark tonal	1 square, 34" x 34"	Backing
Quilt grid	1 square, 28" x 28"	Quilt grid
Batting	1 square, 28" x 28"	Batting

Layer

1. Use a dry iron on a medium setting to fuse the quilt top grid to the batting.

2. Fold the backing fabric in half vertically, then horizontally. Press the creases.

3. Unfold and lay out the backing fabric wrong side up. Spray the wrong side of the backing fabric with temporary spray adhesive to make it tacky.

4. Fold the grid/batting sandwich in half. Center it grid side up on the backing fabric; an even amount of backing should show all the way around the grid/batting. Smooth the grid/batting sandwich in place, and secure it to the backing fabric.

5. Mark an X on the center of the grid. Spray the grid with temporary spray adhesive.

◀ 6. Fold the center square in half vertically and horizontally to locate the center of the block. Match the center of the center square with the center of the grid, and smooth out any wrinkles as shown. Dab fabric glue on each of the four corners of the center square to help it adhere to the grid.

7. Create single-fold strips for the first and second borders. For detailed instructions, refer to One Stitch Strips in Part 1.

Arrange

1. Place the first border strip so the strip's fold is at the top of the block. The raw edge of the border strip should extend past the raw side edge of the center square by ¼". Once you are satisfied with the strip's position, cut it to 18½". Add a little fabric glue to the border strip; finger press the strip in place.

2. Repeat Step 1 for the first border at the bottom of the center square.

◀ 3. Place the folded edge of another first border strip at the right side of the center square; overlap the strips on the top and bottom of the block. Repeat for the first border on the left side of the center square. Cut each side strip so its top edge is even with the top edge of the top strip and its bottom edge is even with the bottom edge of the bottom strip as shown. Add a little fabric glue to the border strip; finger press the strip in place.

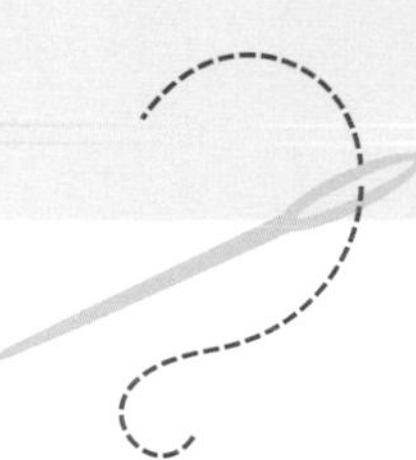

4. Starting at the top of the quilt top, place the second border strip so its folded side overlaps the raw edge of the first border by ¼". Extend the end of the strip to the edge of the grid at the 24" line, and cut the strip even with the 24" grid line. Repeat for the bottom border strip. Glue both border strips in place.

5. Place the folded edge of another second border strip at the right side of the wall hanging; overlap the raw edges of the first border. Extend the ends of the strip across the top and bottom border strips. Cut the strip so it is even with the outside edges of the top and bottom borders.

6. Repeat Step 5 for the second border on the left side of the wall hanging.

7. Fold under a corner of the right border at the bottom of the wall hanging. Finger press the folded corner to create a mitered border.

8. Fuse or glue the miter underneath the border.

9. Repeat Steps 7 and 8 for the top of the right border and the top and bottom of the left border.

10. Fold each corner of the backing fabric once toward each corner of the batting. Press.

11. Fold each corner of the backing fabric toward each corner of the batting a second time. Press.

12. Fold each side of the backing fabric once once toward the center so the raw edge of the fabric is even with the edge of the batting. Press.

13. Add a strip of fusible tape along the outside edge of each side of the backing fabric.

14. Fold each side of the backing fabric once more so the folded edge of the backing covers the raw edge of the second border, and fuse the fabric in place. If desired, use No. 2 safety pins to pin through all of the layers of the quilt with safety pins.

Stitch

1. Replace the sewing machine's presser foot with a walking foot. Set the machine to a small zigzag stitch with a width of no more than 3.5 and a length of 2.5.

2. Stitch down the first border of one side of the quilt. Repeat for remaining sides of the quilt.

3. Make four envelope roses. For detailed instructions, refer to One Stitch Embellishments in Part 1. Place an envelope rose in each corner of the wall hanging; keep the raw edges beneath the mitered border.

4. Stitch the second and outside borders. If desired, avoid stitching over the mitered edge at the top to provide a built-in hanging sleeve for the wall hanging.

5. If desired, free-motion quilt the borders and around the motifs of the center square.

Variation: Picket Fence Wall Hanging

Finished Size: 21" x 21"

Take a simple wall hanging from fun to funky with a trio of embellishments.

Large-scale chenille rickrack, chunky multicolored yarn and 1"-wide grosgrain ribbon add dimension and texture to the Picket Fence Wall Hanging. If you want to try this look, add 2½ yd. chenille rickrack, 1½ yd. grosgrain ribbon and 1 small skein of chunky yarn to your shopping list.

Substitute the Picket Fence large Art to Sew Block or another printed panel of your choice for the Rose Arbor block. Assemble the quilt layers and center block as directed in the Rose Arbor Wall Quilt.

Next, add yarn loops across the bottom of the center block. Position the loops so the single-fold border will help conceal the stitching and the bottom edges of the yarn loops. For detailed instructions to create and add yarn loop trim, refer to One Stitch Embellishments in Part 1.

Add a single-fold border strip around the center square; be sure the bottom strip covers the bottom edge of the yarn loop trim. Trim the quilt sandwich so the top, batting, backing fabric and grid all are the same size.

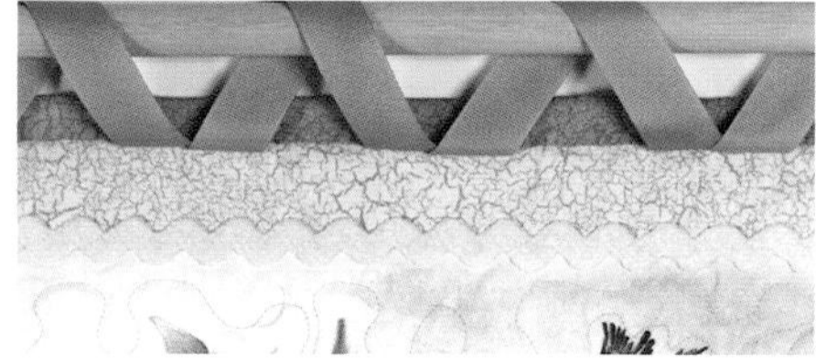

Before you stitch the double-load strip to the top edge of the quilt, add the grosgrain ribbon hanging loops. Refer to One Stitch Finishes in Part 1 for detailed instructions. Finish the piece by adding a narrow double-load strip to each edge of the wall hanging and free-motion quilting around the elements of the art block.

Buttons and Blooms Wall Quilt

Finished Size: 23" x 25"

Make your own everlasting bouquet with the Buttons and Blooms Wall Quilt. Whether you love roses or other posies, head to your fabric store to pick the perfect flowers. Fussy cut a mix of leaves, buds and blooms to add variety, then add them to the appliquéd basket covered with twining vines. Finish off the quilt with a pair of buttons. Go through your own collection to find the right shank-style buttons for the job, or hunt at your favorite antique shop or retailer.

Materials

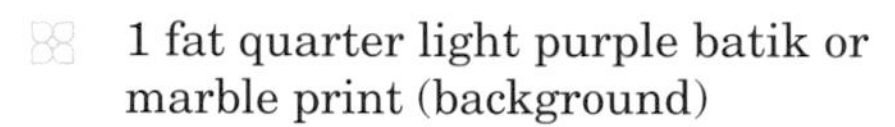

- 1 fat quarter light purple batik or marble print (background)
- 1 yd. small-scale purple floral (second border)
- 1 fat quarter dark green solid (vine stems)
- 1 fat quarter brown basket print (basket, handle)
- 1 yd. medium to dark purple solid to coordinate with purple floral (backing/binding, first border)
- ½ yd. large-scale floral fabric that features at least three different flowers, or coordinating florals of your choice (fussy-cut flowers for basket)
- 1 yd. fusible web
- 1 spool of coordinating thread
- 1 yd. cotton batting
- 1 package fusible quilt grid
- 2 shank-style buttons, 1" diameter
- 1 nylon pressing bar
- Rose Basket pattern pieces on page 118
- Sewing tools and supplies

From	Cut	For
Light purple batik	1 rectangle, 14½" x 17½"	Background
Purple solid	1 rectangle, 25" x 27" 2 strips, 2½" x 42"	Backing First border
Purple floral	4 strips, 6½" x 42"	Second border
Quilt top grid	1 rectangle, 23" x 25"	Grid
Batting	1 rectangle, 23" x 25"	Batting

Layer

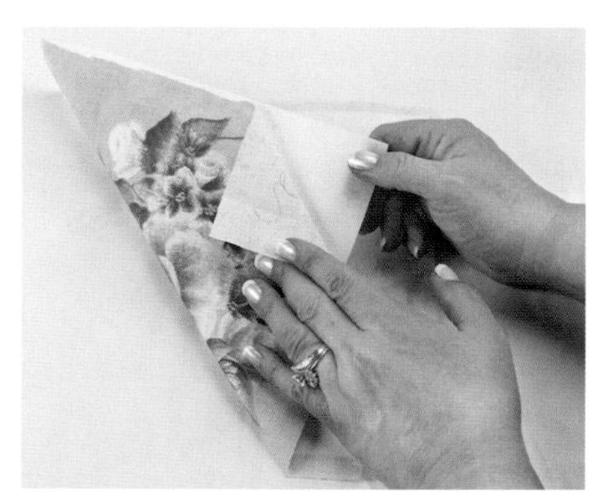

1. Place the desired floral print on the fusible web. You can use a roughly basket-sized bouquet from a single print or pick and choose coordinating florals to piece together in the basket. Be sure to choose fabric that features at least three different styles of flowers that will coordinate, and at least a half-dozen separate flowers plus leaves. Fuse the fabric to the web. Leave the paper backing in place.

2. Fussy cut the fused floral and leaf motifs. Cut out three to five flowers in at least three different motifs and as many leaves as possible in a variety of shapes and sizes.

3. Trace the basket and basket handle patterns on the fusible web.

4. Cut out the pattern pieces. Leave the paper backing in place.

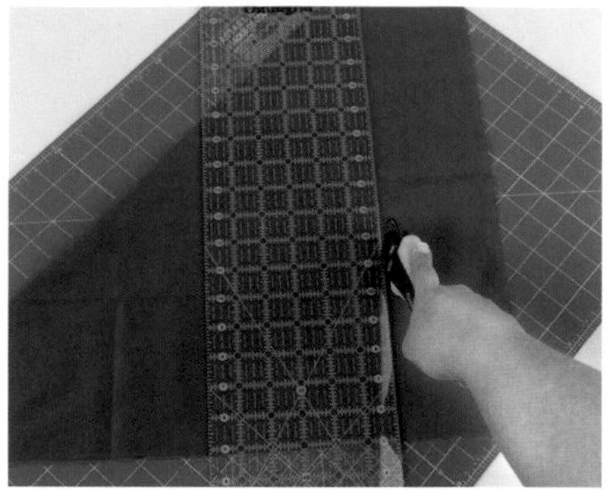

5. Fold the dark green fat quarter on the diagonal, wrong sides together. Press the crease. Unfold the fat quarter, and cut it apart on the crease line.

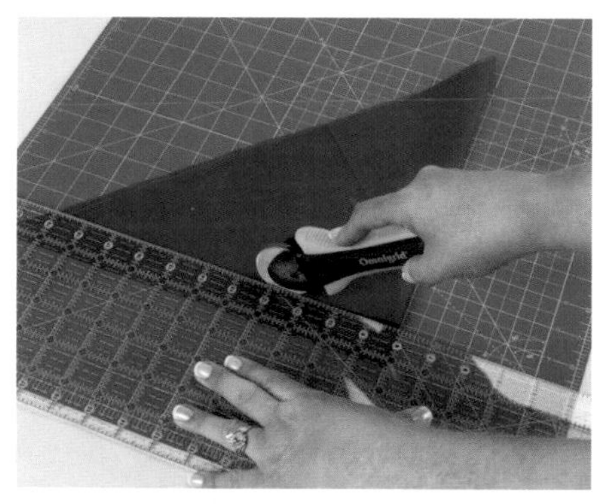

6. Refold one of the triangles in half, wrong sides together. Cut two strips, each 1¼" wide.

7. Fold each strip in half vertically, wrong sides together. Stitch each strip using a ¼" seam allowance. Trim the seam to ⅛".

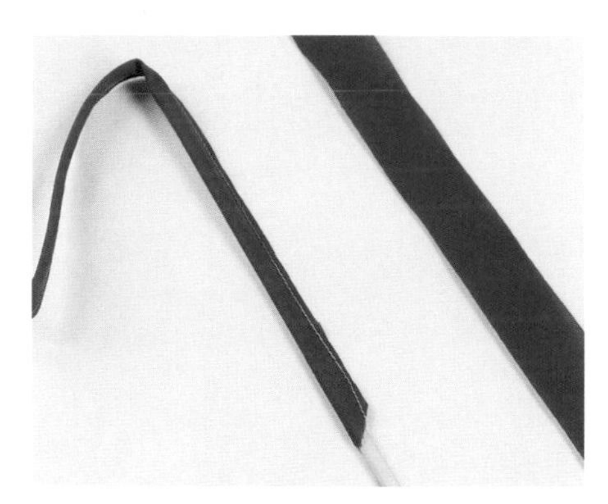

8. Slide a nylon pressing bar into the tube created in Step 7.

9. Press the seam allowance under to create a bias strip.

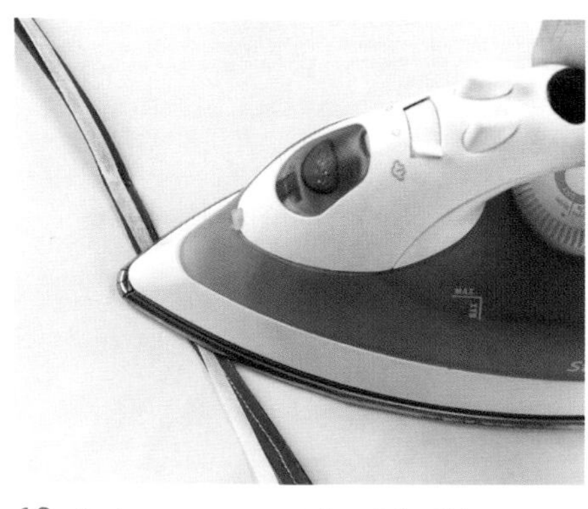

10. Cut a narrow strip of fusible tape. Fuse it to the back of the vine strip.

11. Use a dry iron on a medium setting to fuse the quilt top grid to the batting.

12. Fold the backing fabric in half vertically, then horizontally. Press the creases.

13. Unfold the backing fabric and lay it out wrong side up. Spray the wrong side of the backing fabric with temporary spray adhesive to make it tacky.

14. Fold the grid/batting sandwich in half. Center it grid side up on the backing fabric; an even amount of backing should show all the way around the grid/batting. Smooth the grid/batting sandwich in place, and secure it to the backing fabric.

15. Spray the grid with temporary spray adhesive.

16. Create single-fold strips for the first and second borders. For detailed instructions, refer to One Stitch Strips in Part 1.

Arrange

1. Fold the background square in half twice. Press to mark the creases.

2. Fold the fusible basket in half; mark the center point. Place the center of basket on the center of the backing about 2½" from the bottom of the rectangle. Add the basket handle; tuck the raw edges under the basket.

3. Remove the paper backing from the fussy-cut flowers and leaves. Arrange them as desired in the basket.

4. Cut seven strips, each 2" long, from the green bias strips. Wrap the 2" strips around the basket handle at equal intervals. You can use the metal end of a seam ripper to help you position the strips as desired.

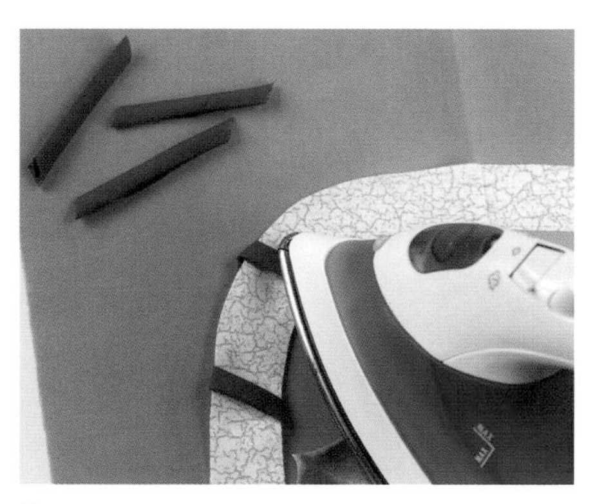

5. Once the basket is arranged as desired, press the fusible pieces in place on the background block to finish the center square.

6. Position the fused basket center square in the center of the fusible grid. Add the first single-fold border, placing the top and bottom strips on first with the folded edge up to the edge of the background block. Add the side strips; place them over the top of the top and bottom strips. Repeat for the second border.

7. Create a double-fold border finish from the backing fabric. For detailed instructions, see One Stitch Finishes in Part 1. If desired, pin the layers in place.

Stitch

1. Beginning in the center and working your way out, stitch through all of the layers around the basket, flowers, leaves and vines. Use a decorative stitch, such as a zigzag, serpentine, blanket or feather stitch.

2. Use a narrow zigzag stitch to stitch in the ditch in the borders.

Sweet Springtime Jacket

Enjoy the beauty of your own flower garden all year with this patchwork mosaic jacket. A few cuts transform a ready-made sweatshirt into a flattering jacket. Appliqué a few fussy-cut floral motifs, then fill in the jacket with shaped patches and lace trim. Chenille rickrack, fabric trim and quilting add fashionable finishing touches.

Materials

- 5 Picket Fence collection Art to Sew blocks (2 Iris Bundle, 1 Hollyhock Bundle, 1 Wisteria Wreath and 1 Morning Glory Wreath); or 2 fat quarters of large-scale floral print; or enough fabric for 5 One Stitch blocks of your choice
- 1½ yd. yellow fern print (placket, cuffs, button loop, large triangles)
- ½ yd. violet fern for (cuffs, bottom trim)
- 1 fat quarter purple sponge or batik print (large squares, small squares)
- 1 fat quarter green sponge or batik print (small triangles)
- 1 off-white sweatshirt with set-in sleeves, one size larger than the wearer usually uses*
- 1½ yd. or 1 package of fusible web
- 6 yd. fusible tape, ½" wide
- 3 yd. cream-colored flat lace
- 3 yd. lilac-colored large chenille rickrack
- 1 shank-style button, 1" diameter
- Sewing tools and supplies
- Thread in cream, lilac and a color to complement the finished quilted design

*NOTE: Once the ribbing is removed, the width of the sweatshirt will shrink.

From	Cut	For
Yellow fern	2 strips, 6" x 42" 1 strip, 2½" x 42" 1 strip, 2½" x 5" 6 strips, 6" x 18"	2 double-fold tuck strips for front plackets 1 single-fold strip for cuffs 1 triple-fold strip for button loop Large triangles
Violet fern	3 strips, 6" x 42"	1 double-fold tuck strip for cuffs and 2 double-fold tuck strips for placket
Purple sponge	3 strips, 4" x 20"	Squares
Green sponge	3 strips, 4" x 20"	Small triangles

Tip

When selecting fabrics to go with whatever color of sweatshirt you choose, follow these basic rules:

- Make sure the fabric for the placket and large triangles closely matches the sweatshirt color.
- The fabric for the cuffs should contrast with the sweatshirt.
- The fabrics for the small triangles and squares should contrast with the large triangles, because the smaller pieces will move the viewer's eye around the shirt and add the zing to the design.

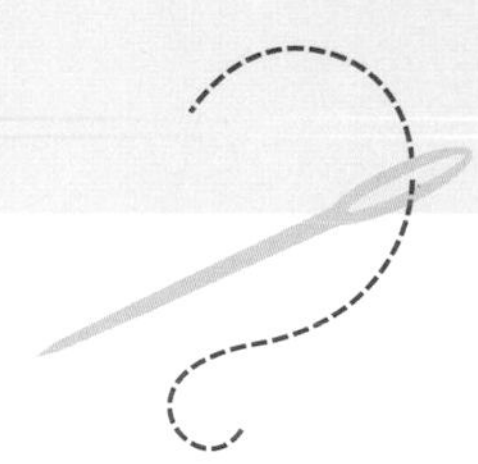

Layer

1. Make the One Stitch strips needed for the project. For detailed instructions, see One Stitch Basics in Part 1.

2. Cut the finished yellow fern single-fold strips in half to yield two equal strips for two cuffs.

3. Cut two finished violet fern double-fold tuck strips in half to yield four equal strips: two for the trim on the cuffs and two for the trim on the bottom front of the sweatshirt.

4. Fuse six yellow fern 6" x 18" strips, three purple sponge 4" x 20" strips and three green sponge 4" x 20" strips to the double-sided fusible web.

5. Cut each yellow fern fused strip into three squares each, 6" x 6". Cut each 6" x 6" square twice on the diagonal to yield four triangles per square, or 72 triangles total. Divide the triangles into two piles of 36 triangles each.

6. Cut each purple sponge fused strip into five squares each, 4" x 4". Cut each 4" x 4" square to yield four squares, 2" x 2", or 60 squares total. Divide the squares into two piles of 27 squares each and set aside six squares. From the remaining six squares, cut each square in quarters to yield four small squares, 1" x 1", per square, or 24 small squares total.

7. Cut each green sponge fused strip into five squares, 4" x 4". Cut each 4" x 4" square twice on the diagonal to yield four triangles, or 60 triangles total. Divide the triangles into two piles of 30 squares each.

8. Fuse the Art to Sew blocks or large-scale floral motifs onto double-sided fusible web. Use an iron on a steam setting to fuse the web to the back of the fabric; follow the manufacturer's directions. Fussy cut the motifs; leave the paper backing in place. Set two matching motifs aside for the front of the jacket; set the three remaining motifs aside for the back of the jacket.

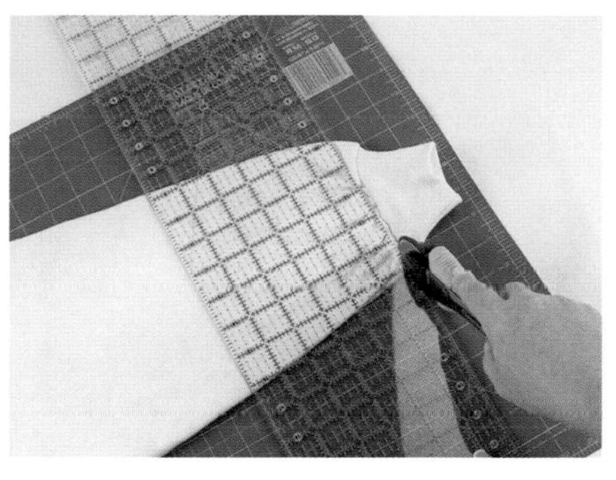

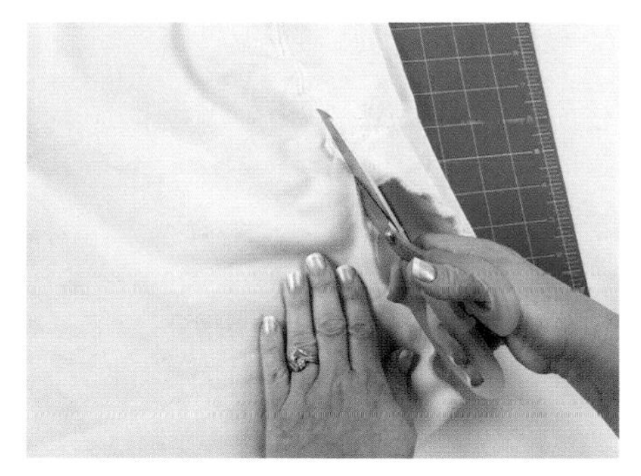

9. Cut the ribbing off the cuffs and bottom of the sweatshirt. Keep the cut edges as even as possible.

10. Measure the front of the sweatshirt across the center, just under the armholes. Find the center of this measurement, and mark it from the collar to the bottom of the sweatshirt.

◀ 11. Fold the sweatshirt in half on the center line; be sure to bring the shoulder seams together. Press the crease line on front of the shirt as shown. Many sweatshirts are made from one continuous tube of fabric. If there is no seam under the arms of the sweatshirt, press a crease line under each arm.

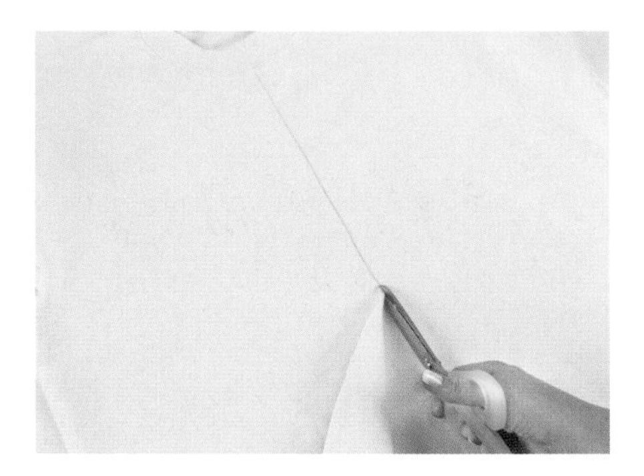

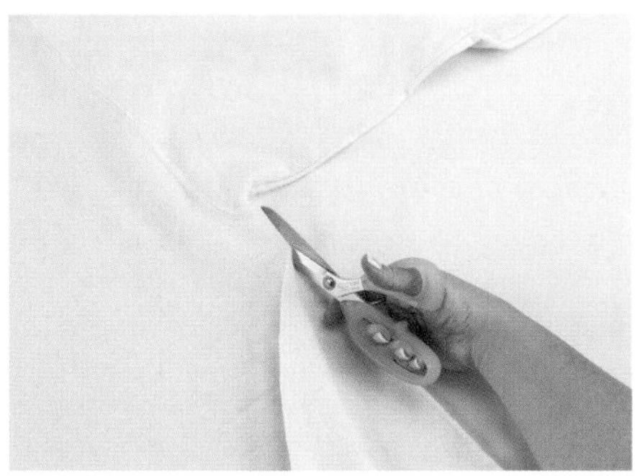

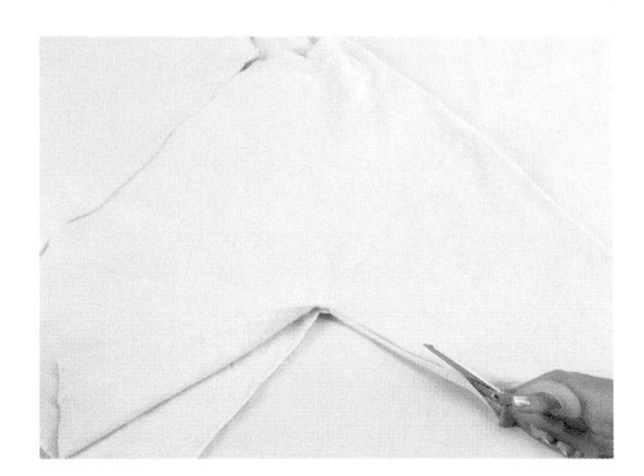

12. Cut the front of sweatshirt open on the marked, creased line.

13. Cut open the sides of the sweatshirt under the arms along each seamline or crease line. Cut through the armhole to open the seam of the sleeve. Lay the sweatshirt out on the table. The shirt should lay completely flat with the arms, back and two sides open to work on.

Arrange

1. Begin arranging the large triangles in a random fashion, 1" away from the cut edges of the two front sides of the sweatshirt. Remove the paper backing from each triangle before putting it in place on the sweatshirt.

2. Center one large floral motif 6" from the bottom edge of the sweatshirt.

3. Place one large triangle under the floral motif to give the impression of a pot. Center one small triangle on top of a large triangle. Add onc small square at the point of the small triangle. Add two small triangles to the base of the large triangle to give the impression of feet on the pot. Repeat for the other side of the sweatshirt front.

4. Arrange the small triangles randomly on the front sides of the sweatshirt; rcmovc the backing as you go. Overlap large triangles and fill in the gaps as shown. Add large squares in a random fashion, removing the backing as you go. Strive to get the corners of the large squares to touch and overlap the two sizes of triangles. Sprinkle in small squares anywhere the design needs some zing; remove the backing as you go. Repeat for the other side of the sweatshirt front.

5. Once you are satisfied with the design, steam press all of the pieces to each side of the sweatshirt front.

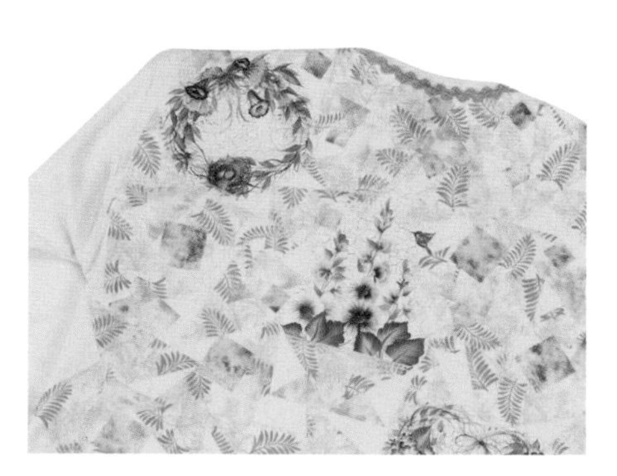

6. Remove the backing from each of the large floral motifs. Place one large floral motif 4" from the bottom right-hand edge of the back of the sweatshirt. Place a large floral motif in the upper left hand corner, about 1" from the shoulder seam. Place a large floral motif in the center of the back of the sweatshirt to form a diagonal line of three floral motifs as shown. Feel free to place your motifs in another pattern as desired. Add the large triangles in a random fashion, 1" from the cut edges of the back of the sweatshirt; overlap the large triangles across the shoulder seams. Continue to place the large triangles, small triangles, large squares and small squares on the back of the sweatshirt as you did for the front of the sweatshirt. Steam press all of the pieces to the sweatshirt once you are satisfied with the design.

Stitch

1. While the sweatshirt is still flat, use a complementary thread to free-motion quilt over all of the pieces. Add strips of flat lace as desired. Be sure your stitching covers the sweatshirt and catches each piece as you go.

2. Fold the neckline ribbing in half toward the right side of the sweatshirt. Use the cream thread to stitch the ribbing in place.

3. Place rickrack along the bottom edge of the folded neckline ribbing. Use the lilac thread to stitch the rickrack in place.

◀ 4. Fold and press the violet fern double-tuck strips in half. Press ½"-wide fusible tape to the wrong side of the strip on both long sides. Starting with the front of the sweatshirt, wrap trim around the bottom edge of the sweatshirt as shown. Place the sweatshirt edge against the folded crease line of the double-tuck strip. Steam press the tape in place from both sides of the sweatshirt. Use a zigzag stitch to sew down the bottom trim. Make sure the stitch is wide enough to catch both sides of the trim strip. Repeat for the second front edge and the back edge of the sweatshirt.

5. Lay one yellow fern single-fold strip so it is 1" above the bottom edge of each cuff, and so the raw edge of the strip is toward the raw edge of the cuff. Fold and press the violet fern double-tuck cuff strips in half. Slip a strip beneath the edge of each cuff.

6. Flip the strip up to cover the raw edge of the yellow fern strip. Lay a strip of rickrack over the overlapped strips. Stitch the strips and trim together in one stitch. Repeat for the other cuff.

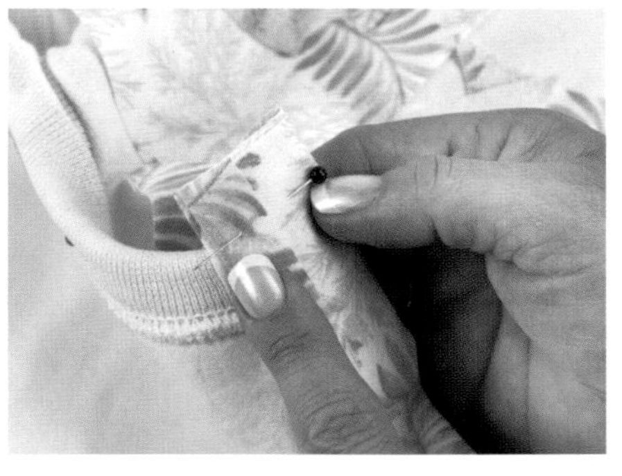

7. Fold and press the yellow fern double-tuck strips in half. Press ½"-wide fusible tape to the wrong side of the strip on both long sides. Starting 1" above the ribbed neckline of one front side of the sweatshirt, place the sweatshirt edge against the folded crease line of the double-tuck strip, and run the trim along the front placket.

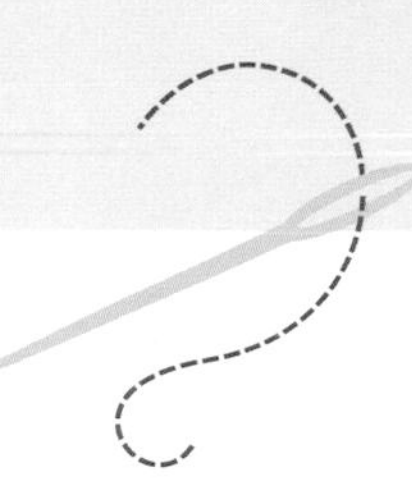

8. Extend the strip 1" below the bottom edge trim of the sweatshirt. Remove the backing and steam press the trim from the center of the double-tuck strip to about 10" on either side. Press both sides of the sweatshirt to hold the trim in place. Repeat for the other placket edge.

9. Fold the top edge of the double-tuck strip right sides together, against itself. Sew it in place close to the neckline. Trim the seam to ⅛". Turn the trim edging right side out to the front of the sweatshirt. Repeat for the bottom of the placket trim strip to ensure all of the raw edges are covered.

10. Reassemble the main body of the sweatshirt. Position the sections right sides together; pin if desired. Use a ½" seam allowance to sew one side seam; start sewing 6" above the bottom trim, and stop sewing at the edge of the sleeve. Repeat for the other side seam. Press the seams open. There will be a split, or vent, at the bottom of the sweatshirt.

11. At the vent at the bottom of the sweatshirt, fold and pin ½" to 1" of fleece wrong sides together on each side of the split to create a folded edge. Use cream-colored thread to stitch the folded edge in place. Repeat for each vent edge.

12. Pin or fuse the ends of the cuffs right sides together. Slide the sleeve, wrong side out, onto the free arm of the machine. Stitch the cuff and lower sleeve with a ½" seam.

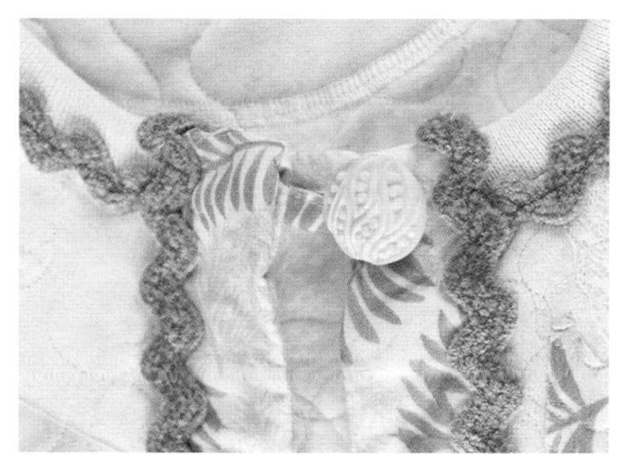

13. Crisscross the ends of the button loop strip. Place the loop under the placket on the top right side of the sweatshirt. Stitch the loop down through the placket to anchor it; the trim will hide the stitching. Position the button on the opposite side placket, and sew it in place.

Pocket Full of Posies Tote

Finished Size: 17" x 17"

Both pretty and practical, this roomy tote will quickly become your favorite for running errands, heading to the gym or taking in a quilting class. Four pockets — two outside and two inside — make it easy to stay organized. Padded straps give your hands and shoulders a break, and they wrap all the way around the tote to provide extra strength.

Materials

- 7/8 yd. prequilted cotton cream solid with batting on one side and quilted fabric on the other (inside of bag)
- 5/8 yd. green fern print (outside of bag)
- 2 Art to Sew squares (Wisteria Wreath and Morning Glory Wreath) from the Picket Fence collection, or 2 squares of a large-scale floral print (outside pockets)
- 1/2 yd. small-scale violet floral print (ruffle)
- 1/2 yd. green crackle or tonal print (straps)
- 1/2 yd. small-scale green floral (trim strips for outside pockets, inside pockets, grid cover)
- 4" x 13" piece of plastic canvas
- 5 yd. narrow ribbon
- Thread to coordinate with project
- Sewing tools and supplies

From	Cut	For
Prequilted cream solid	1 strip, 20" x 32" 2 squares, 9" x 9"	Tote lining Exterior pockets
Green fern	1 strip, 20" x 32" 2 squares, 9" x 9"	Tote exterior Exterior pocket lining
Art to Sew squares/large-scale floral	2 squares, 9" x 9"; center the motif on the square, then square up each piece to 9" x 9"	Exterior pockets
Violet floral	4 strips, 4" x 42"	Ruffle
Green crackle	3 strips, 4" x 42"	Straps
Green floral	2 strips, 3" x 42" 4 squares, 9" x 9"' 1 rectangle, 10" x 15"	Triple-fold trim strips Interior pockets Grid pocket

Layer and Arrange

1. Prepare the triple-fold trim strips. For detailed instructions, refer to One Stitch Basics in Part 1.

2. Lay out the 9" x 9" exterior pocket lining square wrong side up. Spray the lining square with temporary adhesive. Lay the prequilted square fabric batting side up on the lining square. Spray the batting side of the 9" x 9" prequilted square. Place the 9" x 9" Art to Sew or large-scale floral square right side up on top of the prequilted square. If desired, pin through all three layers to hold them together. Repeat for the other exterior pocket.

3. Spray the batting side of the prequilted fabric with temporary spray adhesive. Lay the green fern print tote exterior right side up on top of the prequilted fabric.

4. Use fusible tape to secure the tote exterior fabric around the edges.

Stitch

1. Use a ½" seam allowance to sew a pair of 4" violet floral strips together on the short sides. Press the strips in half lengthwise, wrong sides together. You should have two strips. Set the sewing machine to the widest zigzag setting; usually it's a setting of 6 for both width and length.

◀ 2. Place the narrow ribbon ½" from the raw edge of the folded strip. Zigzag stitch over the ribbon without catching it in the stitching as shown. Leave a tail of ribbon at each end of the strip.

3. Place a safety pin at one end of the strip to secure the tail. Pull on the other end of the ribbon to gather the strip and fit it to the top of the bag. You will need two 20" ruffle strips.

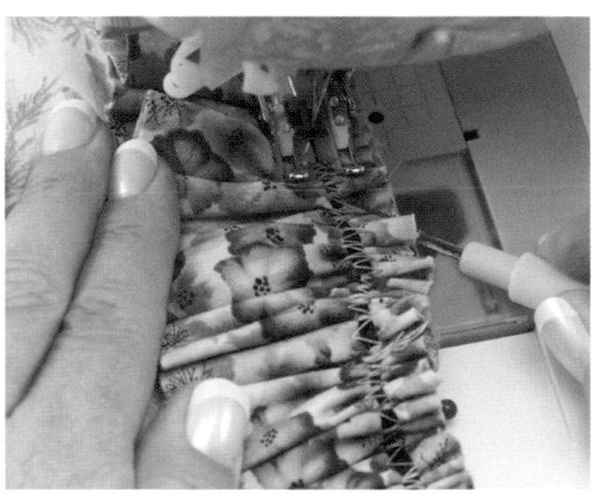

4. Place the gathered ruffle right sides together, even with the raw edge of one short side of the tote bag exterior fabric. Stitch down the ruffle through the gathering ribbon to anchor it in place.

5. Repeat for the other end of the tote bag exterior fabric.

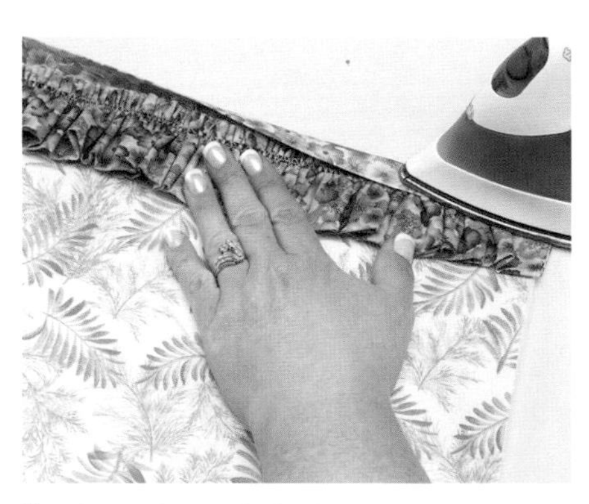

6. Place the folded edge of a green floral trim strip over the raw edges of the ruffle/bag. Fold the trim strip to the inside of the bag. Use ½"-wide fusible tape to hold the strip in place.

7. Stitch the trim strip down, covering the zigzag stitching of the ruffle and the raw edges of the tote bag. At this point the ruffle will be right side up against the bag, and the trim strip will be at what will be the top of the bag.

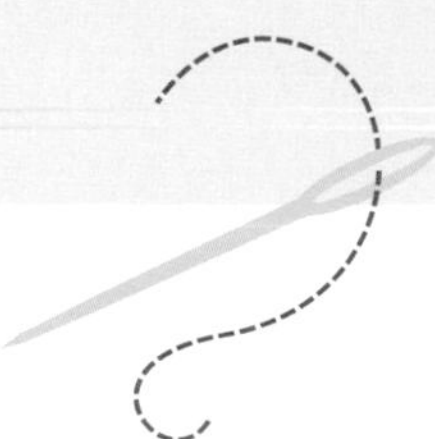

8. Turn the trim strip down to the inside of the bag. Stitch the seam down from the outside of the bag.

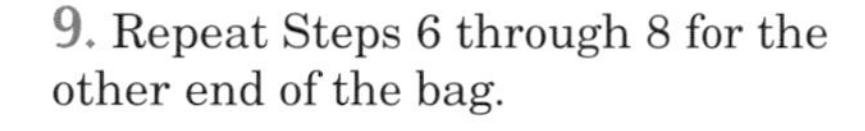

9. Repeat Steps 6 through 8 for the other end of the bag.

10. Place a green floral triple-fold trim strip on the top and bottom edge of each exterior pocket; use ½"-wide fusible tape to hold the strip in place. Use a single line of zigzag stitching along the bottom edge of the top strip and along the top edge of the bottom strip to secure each strip. Trim each strip so it is even with the raw edges of the pocket layers. Repeat for the other pocket.

11. Place two 9" green floral interior pocket squares right sides together. Use a ¼" seam allowance to stitch around the outside edges of the squares; leave a 4" opening to turn the pockets right side out. Trim the corners of the squares close to the stitching line; avoid cutting into the stitching. Turn the pockets right side out. Press. Repeat for the other interior pocket.

12. Bring the ruffled edges of the bag body together, folding the tote bag in half with the right sides of the exterior fabric together. Press a crease line at the fold to mark the center of the bottom of the bag. Fold the bag body in half lengthwise, right sides together. Press the crease line to mark the long center line of the bag.

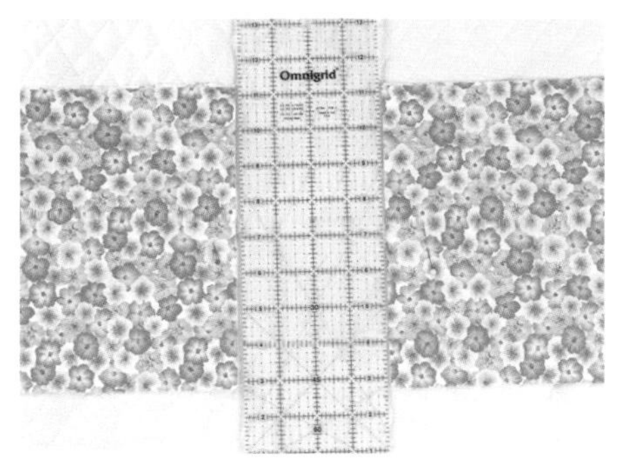

13. Lay the bag body out flat, wrong side up. Measure 2" from the short crease line. Center the inside pockets on the long crease lines. Pin the pockets in place through all of the thicknesses. Use a zigzag stitch to sew down the bottom of each pocket from the right side of the bag.

14. Repeat Step 13 for the exterior pocket, except place the bag right side up. Zigzag stitch each exterior pocket along the lower edge of the lower piece of the trim strip to secure it to the tote.

15. Use a diagonal seam to join the 4"-wide strips for the tote bag straps into one long strip that measures roughly 110" long. Stitch a diagonal seam to join the two ends of the long strip into a tube.

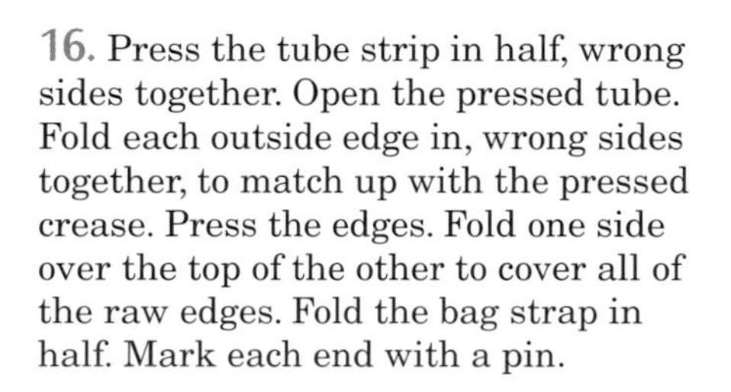

16. Press the tube strip in half, wrong sides together. Open the pressed tube. Fold each outside edge in, wrong sides together, to match up with the pressed crease. Press the edges. Fold one side over the top of the other to cover all of the raw edges. Fold the bag strap in half. Mark each end with a pin.

◀ 17. Place the bag strap on either side of the exterior pockets; cover ½" of the raw edge. Match each pin with the center bottom crease line. Equally divide the strap between the two sides of the pocket. Use ½"-wide fusible tape on the wrong side of the strap, and press it into place before you stitch.

◀ 18. Use a straight stitch to sew the strap in place as shown. Begin stitching ½" from the ruffled edge at the top of the bag on the inside of the strap, and continue around the bag until you reach the opposite side of the pocket. Stitch across the strap to the outside edge of the strap, and travel around the outside of the strap until you reach the starting point. Stitch across the strap to secure it.

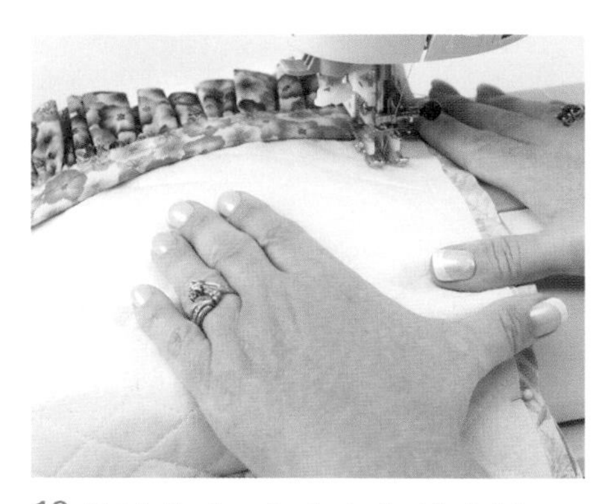

19. Fold the bag body in half, right sides together. Match the top edges, including the ruffles. Use a ½" seam allowance to stitch the sides of the bag together. Use trim strips to cover the raw edges of the seams.

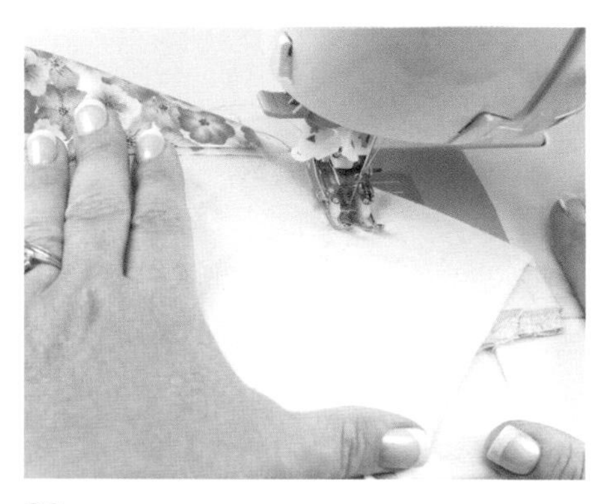

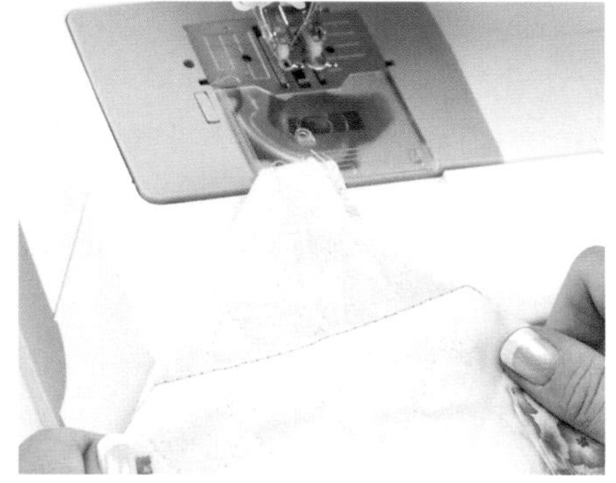

20. Measure up 2" from the bottom of each of the side seams. Fold a seam down to create a triangle. Stitch across the triangle to form the sides and bottom of the tote bag.

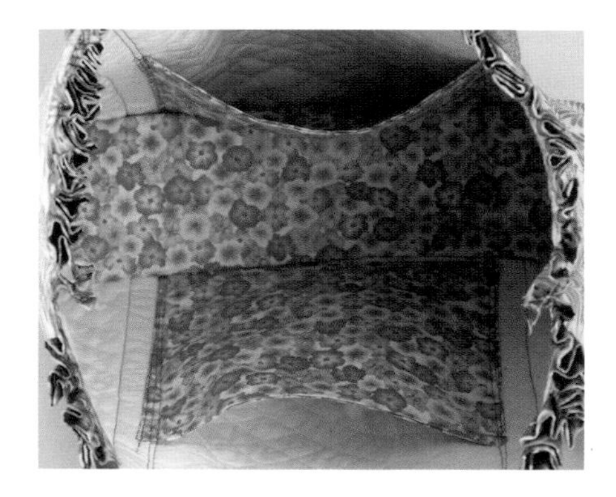

21. Lay the 10" x 14" rectangle out, wrong side up. Fold ½" of each edge toward the center of the fabric. Secure each edge with fusible tape, then topstitch each edge to hold it in place. Wrap the fabric snugly around the plastic canvas grid so the two 13" edges meet up in the middle of one side of the grid. Stitch the ends of the wrapped fabric to secure the grid cover. Place the covered grid, open side down, in the bottom of the tote.

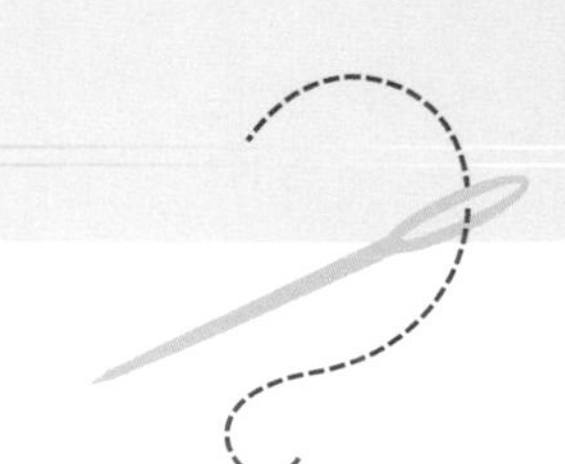

Crazy Patch Purse

Finished Size: 10" x 13"

Make a fashion statement with the colorful fabrics, funky handles and popular patchwork motif featured in the Crazy Patch Purse designed by Julie Massey and Carolyn Bassingthwaighte. Get all of the function you need in a bag that's roomy enough to hold all of your essentials and sturdy enough to stand up to the rigors of everyday use.

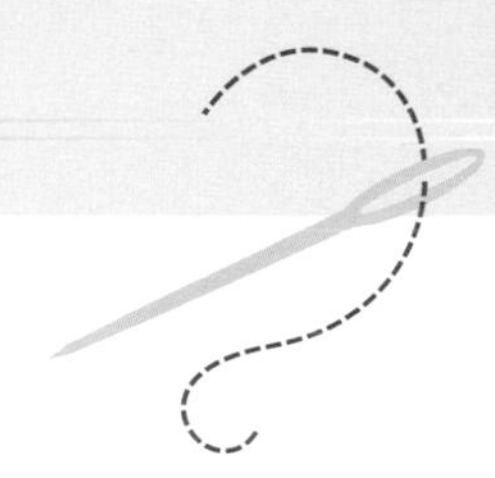

Materials

- ½ yd. purple crackle or tonal print (A, H, handle tabs, purse bottom, purse sides)
- ¼ yd. violet small-scale floral print (B, J)
- ¼ yd. pink crackle or tonal print (C, I)
- ⅛ yd. green fern print (D)
- ¼ yd. hunter green crackle or tonal print (E, G)
- ⅛ yd. green sponge or batik print (F)
- ⅝ yd. purple fern print (backing)
- ½ yd. heavy, double-fusible interfacing*
- 1 package fusible quilt top grid
- Fusible tape, ⅝" wide
- ½ yd. cotton batting
- Pair of coordinating purchased purse handles with slots in the handle ends for attachment
- Thread to match fabric
- Sewing tools and supplies
- Crazy Patch patterns on pages 120 and 121

*NOTE: Fast-2-Fuse interfacing was used for the purse shown.

From	Cut	For
Purple crackle	2 rectangles, 4¼" x 7½" 2 rectangles, 7" x 8" 4 strips, 1½" x 3½" 1 rectangle, 3" x 33"	A H Handle tabs Exterior tote bottom and sides
Violet floral	2 rectangles, 3¼" x 7½" 2 rectangles, 5½" x 6"	B J
Pink crackle	2 rectangles, 5" x 6½" 2 rectangles, 6¾" x 7½"	C I
Green fern	2 rectangles, 4½" x 5½"	D
Hunter green crackle	2 rectangles, 5¼" x 6½" 2 rectangles, 6" x 7"	E G
Green sponge	2 rectangles, 4½" x 7¼"	F
Purple fern	2 rectangles, 15" x 18" 1 rectangle, 8½" x 37"	Backing fabric, tote front and back Interior tote bottom and sides
Interfacing	2 rectangles, 9¾" x 12½" 1 rectangle, 4" x 33"	Tote front and back Tote bottom and sides
Fusible quilt top grid	2 rectangles, 9¾" x 12½"	Tote front and back
Batting	2 rectangles, 9¾" x 12½" 1 rectangle, 4" x 33"	Tote front and back Tote bottom and sides

Layer

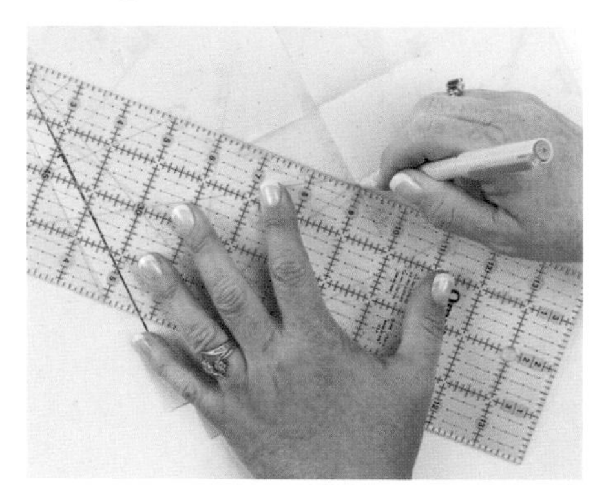

1. Use a permanent ink fabric marker to transfer the Crazy Patch Purse Pattern to each fusible quilt top grid piece.

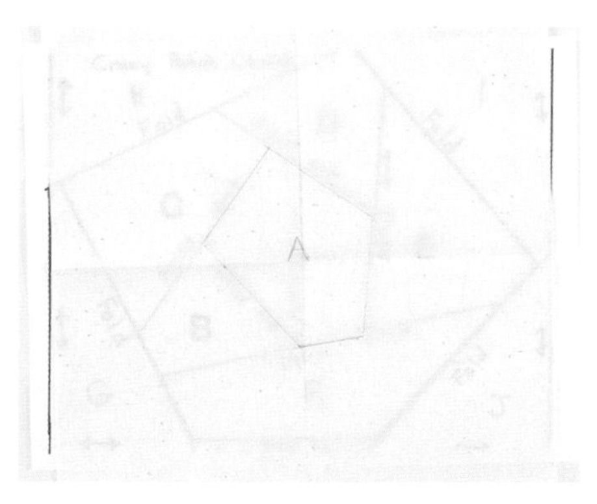

2. Use an iron on a medium setting to press the grid to the corresponding batting piece. Steam press the grid/batting sandwich to the interfacing. Repeat for the second set of grid, batting and interfacing pieces.

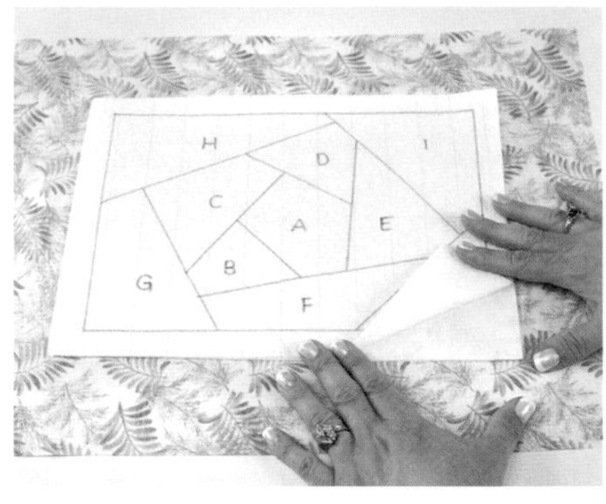

3. Center the grid/batting/interfacing sandwich on the backing fabric. Steam the sandwich and backing to fuse the pieces.

4. Use a steam iron to fuse the bag's side and bottom batting rectangle to the side and bottom interfacing rectangle. Center the batting/interfacing sandwich on the exterior bag bottom and sides backing fabric. Fuse in place. Spray the wrong side of the interior bag bottom and side fabric, and center it on the batting.

5. Create single-fold strips from each of the lettered crazy patch fabric pieces (A through J). For detailed instructions, see One Stitch Basics in Part 1.

6. Spray the inside of the first single-fold strip. Finger press the strip together. Place a small strip of fusible tape on one side of the outside of the quilt piece. Repeat for the remaining single-fold strips.

Arrange

1. Place Piece A, which is the centerpiece, on the grid according to the pattern. Piece A can be placed on the pattern in any direction as long as it overlaps all of the lines. Press Piece A down to hold it in place.

2. Add Piece B to the grid. Keep the folded edge of the fabric on the pattern line. Once you are satisfied with its placement, press Piece B down to hold it in place.

3. Continue to add strips to the grid, proceeding in alphabetical order through the pattern. Remember to keep the folded edge of the fabric on the pattern line and press each piece down once you are satisfied with its placement. You may need to adjust pieces to cover raw edges. Trim away any excess fabric from the edge of the batting.

4. On each short side of the bag's back and front, fold the backing fabric until the raw edge is even with the batting; press the backing to crease it. Fold the backing ¼" away from edge of batting, placing creased edge over the raw edges of the crazy patch quilt center to form a binding. It is important to have the ¼" lip of fabric extending beyond the batting; this is your seam allowance for joining the purse's front and back with the bottom/side strip. Once the fabric is folded, pin it in place. Repeat for the long sides of the bag's front and back, except omit the ¼" lip on the top edge of each piece.

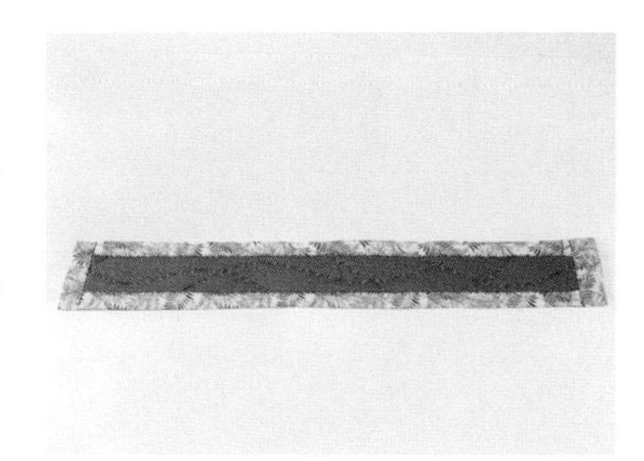

5. Fold the backing fabric for the bottom/side piece as you did for the front and back crazy quilted sections. Start with the long edges; let a ¼" lip of fabric extend beyond the batting. Fold the short ends without the lip.

Stitch

1. Use a variety of your machine's crazy quilt-style stitches to topstitch all of the crazy quilt patchwork pieces and binding edges on the bag's front and back. Stitch crazy quilt stitches randomly across bottom/side strip. Stitch the edge of the binding to secure it.

2. With right sides together, stitch the bag's front to the bottom/side strip. Start at the top of one side and stitch down to the corner. Then start at the top of the other side and stitch the side and bottom, easing as needed for fit. Repeat for the back side.

3. Turn the tote right side out. Shape the corners, sides and bottom as shown.

4. Fold one strip of tab fabric in half lengthwise; press the folded edge. Open the fabric and fold raw edges to the center; press the folds. Refold the strip on the center. Press. Stitch the tab to hold it in place. Repeat for the remaining tabs.

5. Slide one tab through each handle slot. Center the handle on tote front, and mark the placement for each tab. Fold the ends of each tab under and pin them in place. Repeat for the tote back. Stitch around the entire top edge of the bag as shown, catching the handle tabs in the stitches as you sew over them.

Tulip Garden Lap Quilt

Finished Size: 40" x 50"

Enjoy the beauty of your own fabric flower garden with this pretty lap quilt. Patchwork tulip blocks provide a bold punch of color, while printed floral blocks bring a variety of blooms to the mix. For a faster, easier version of the quilt, substitute bold fabric blocks or fussy-cut appliqué blocks for the patchwork tulips.

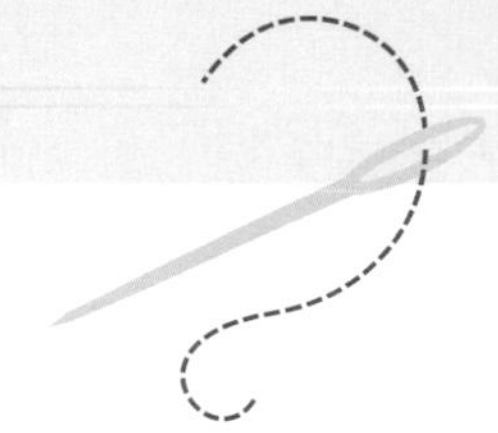

Materials

- 6 Picket Fence collection Art to Sew Blocks (2 Morning Glory Wreath, 2 Wisteria Wreath, 1 Iris Bundle, 1 Hollyhock Bundle); or substitute any 10" x 10" appliqué, patchwork or large-scale fabric from the One Stitch Block Gallery; (adjust fabric requirements as needed)
- ¾ yd. yellow fern print (tulip patchwork background blocks)
- 1 yd. pink crackle or tonal print (tulips, trim strips)
- 1 fat quarter green crackle or tonal print (tulip leaves)
- 1 fat quarter violet small-scale floral (envelope roses)
- 1½ yd. green small-scale floral (backing fabric)
- 2½ yd. hunter green floral (sashing, border)
- 2 packages fusible quilt top grid
- 2 yd. batting
- Sewing tools and supplies

From	Cut	For
Pink crackle	12 squares, 2" x 2" 8 strips, 1½" x 42"	Tulips Trim strips
Yellow fern	6 squares, 10" x 10"	Background for tulip blocks
Violet floral	6 squares, 2" x 2"	Folded roses
Green crackle	6 squares, 2" x 2"	Tulip leaves
Hunter green floral	4 strips, 2½" x 42" 5 strips, 2" x 42" 4 strips, 7¼" x 54"	Single-fold strips for sashing Double-fold strips for sashing Quick-turn strip, double load
Green floral	2 rectangles, 25" x 37" 1 strip, 3" x 42"	Backing fabric Joining strip
Fusible quilt top grid	2 rectangles, 24" x 26"	Quilt top grid
Batting	2 rectangles, 24" x 26" 4 strips, 3" x 54" 4 strips, 2½" x 54"	Quilt top Border strips Border strips

Layer

1. Prepare the trim, single-fold, double-fold, quick-turn and joining strips. For detailed instructions, refer to One Stitch Basics in Part 1.

2. Use a dry iron on a medium setting to fuse one quilt top grid rectangle to one batting rectangle. Repeat for the other pair of rectangles.

3. Lay out both backing fabric sections, wrong side up. Spray the wrong side of the fabric with temporary spray adhesive.

4. Center the batting/grid rectangle on one backing fabric rectangle, batting side down. Allow 1" of backing fabric to show around the batting. Spray the grid with spray adhesive to make it tacky. Repeat for the second set of batting/grid and backing.

Arrange

NOTE: You will be making two rows of the quilt on each grid and batting section. The top half of the quilt is Section 1; the bottom half is Section 2.

1. Make six tulip patchwork blocks. For detailed instructions, refer to the One Stitch Block Gallery in Part 1.

2. Arrange six blocks (three tulip patch blocks and three Art to Sew Blocks) on the Section 1 grid. The raw edges of the blocks should butt against one another, but don't overlap the blocks; the sashing strips will cover the raw edges.

Section 1

Section 2

3. From the 2½"-wide sashing strips cut two strips, each 21" long. From the 2"-wide sashing strips, cut two strips, each 21" long.

4. Place the double-fold 21" sashing strips between the blocks. Place the single-fold 21" sashing strips on the outside edges of the blocks so the raw edges face to the outside of the quilt.

5. Place one long single-fold sashing strip on the top row with the folded side against the raw edge of the blocks. Cut the strip to fit.

6. Place one long double-fold sashing strip between the rows. If desired, use a little fabric glue to secure the ends of the strips.

7. Use No. 2 safety pins to pin baste the section through all thicknesses.

8. Repeat Steps 2 through 7 for Section 2.

Stitch

1. Quilt around the blocks in both of the quilt sections. Use stitches that highlight the motifs, as well as general quilting stitches for the background of each block.

2. Use a narrow zigzag stitch to stitch down the sashing strips between the blocks. Stop stitching 1" away from the bottom of Section 1 and 1" away from the top of Section 2. Starting along the outside of each of the sections, begin stitching with a narrow zigzag stitch. Leave the inside blocks without a sashing strip free from stitching.

3. Use a rotary cutter, large ruler and mat to trim the backing fabric even with the quilt. Press the joining strip in half, wrong sides together. Press a strip of ½"-wide fusible tape on one long side of the strip. Remove the paper backing.

4. Place the joining strip fusible side down and right sides together with the back side of Section 2. The raw edges of the strip should be along the top edge of Section 2. Place the two quilt sections wrong sides together; catch the joining strip, backing, batting and tops of both pieces in a ½" seam. Press the seams to open them.

5. Trim the batting out of the seam to reduce the bulk. Trim the joining strip down to the ¼" seam allowance.

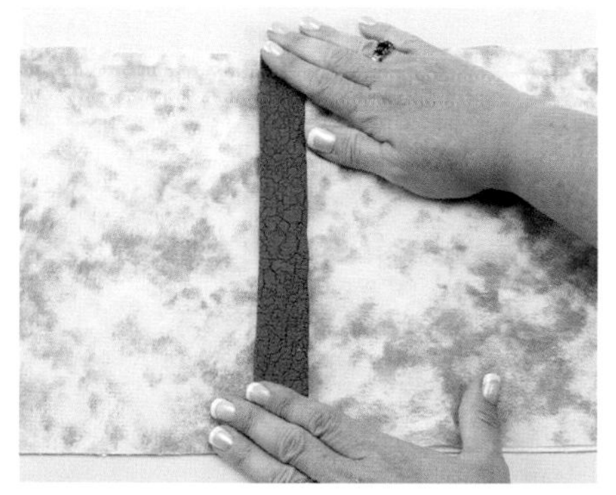

6. Fuse ½"-wide fusible tape under the joining strip on both sides of the seam onto the backing fabric. From the back side of the quilt, open the joining strip so that it covers the joining seam and ½"-wide fusible tape. Press into place.

7. From the front side, place one long double-fold sashing strip between the rows to hide the joining seam allowance. Stitch down the double-fold sashing strip through all of the thicknesses. This stitch will catch the joining strip on the back of the quilt as well.

8. Join two trim strips together, end to end, to make four sets of trim strips. Place the trim strips on the top and bottom of the quilt so the trim strips' raw edges are against the sashing strips' raw edges. Cut the strips to fit. Repeat for the trim strips on the long sides of the quilt.

9. Remove the paper backing from the 7¼"-wide quick-turn strips. Open the strips, and load the 3"-wide batting strips inside, beneath the fold of the strip. The batting will be against the center fold and under the ½" fold of the strip. Load the 2½"-wide strip of batting on top of the first batting strip. This batting will not go beneath the ½" fold of the strip. Overlap the ½" edge of the quick-turn fold strip over the long sides of the quilt. Steam press to hold the strips in place.

10. Stitch down the quick-turn strip to the edge of the quilt. Trim the ends of strips even with the top and bottom edges of the quilt.

11. Repeat Steps 9 and 10 for the opposite side of the quilt.

12. Double load the top and bottom strips; refer to the directions in Step 9 for details. Overlap half of the edge of the quick-turn folded strip over the top and bottom of the quilt.

13. Press the strip into place up to 6" from each corner. Extend the end of the strip 2" past the quilt edge. Fold the ends of the strip up, right sides together. Pin the edges together.

14. Begin stitching in the middle of the strip, and backstitch to the edge. Continue stitching again to the top of the strip. Backstitch and cut the threads. Avoid catching the edge of the quilt when stitching.

15. Trim the corner. Turn the quick-turn strip back to cover the unfinished edge of the quilt. Stitch down the quick-turn strip to the edge of the quilt as shown.

Windows With a View Wall Quilt

Finished Size: 40" x 50"

Give any room a grand view with this classic attic windows design. Ledges and mitered-corner sashing strips help to frame out the scenes and provide a three-dimensional depth to each pane of the quilt.

Materials

- 5 small Garden Path Art to Sew blocks (2 Pansies, 1 Echinacea Bundle, 1 Flower Pots and 1 Thistle Bundle), or any appliqué, patchwork or large-scale fabric you desire from the One Stitch Block Gallery (adjust fabric requirements as needed)
- 1 large Garden Path Art to Sew block (Garden Path), or any appliqué, or large-scale fabric block you desire from the One Stitch Block Gallery
- 1 yd. purple fern print (background)
- ⅓ yd. violet sponge or batik print (sashing)
- ⅓ yd. grass green crackle or tonal print (sashing)
- 1¾ yd. purple crackle or tonal print (backing)
- ⅛ yd. violet small-scale floral print (envelope roses)
- ⅛ yd. pink crackle or tonal print (envelope roses)
- ⅛ yd. green sponge or batik print (folded rosebuds)
- 1¼ yd. cotton batting
- 1 package fusible quilt top grid
- Coordinating thread
- 8 yd. fusible tape, ½" wide
- Sewing tools and supplies

From	Cut	For
Small printed fabric blocks	5 squares, 10" x 10"	Small attic windows blocks
Large printed fabric block	1 square, 20" x 20"	Large attic window block
Purple fern	4 strips, 7" x 42"	Miter-fold strips for border
Violet sponge	2 strips, 4½" x 42"; cut both strips again to measure 4½" x 30½"; trim the remainder of one strip to measure 4½" x 10½"	Single-fold strips for blocks
Grass green crackle	2 strips, 4½" x 42"; cut one strip again to measure 4½" x 20½"; trim the remainder of that strip into two strips, 4½" x 10½"; cut the other strip into three strips, 4½" x 10½"	Miter-fold strips for blocks
Purple crackle	4 strips, 1¾" x 42" 1 square, 42" x 42" 4 strips, 3" x 42"	Single-fold strips for sashing Backing Quick-turn strips for binding
Violet floral	6 squares, 2" x 2"	Envelope roses
Green sponge	4 squares, 2" x 2"	Folded rosebuds
Pink crackle	6 squares, 2" x 2"	Envelope roses
Fusible quilt top grid	1 square, 40" x 40"	Quilt top grid
Batting	1 square, 40" x 40"	Batting

Layer

1. Prepare the single-fold, miter-fold and quick-turn strips. For detailed instructions, refer to One Stitch Basics in Part 1.

2. Use a dry iron on a medium setting to fuse the quilt top grid to the batting.

3. Fold the backing fabric in half vertically, then horizontally. Press the creases. Unfold the backing fabric and lay it out wrong side up. Spray the wrong side of the backing fabric with temporary spray adhesive to make it tacky.

4. Fold the grid/batting sandwich in half. Center it grid side up on the backing fabric; 1" of backing should show all the way around the grid/batting. Smooth the grid/batting sandwich in place, and secure it to the backing fabric. Spray the grid with temporary spray adhesive.

Arrange

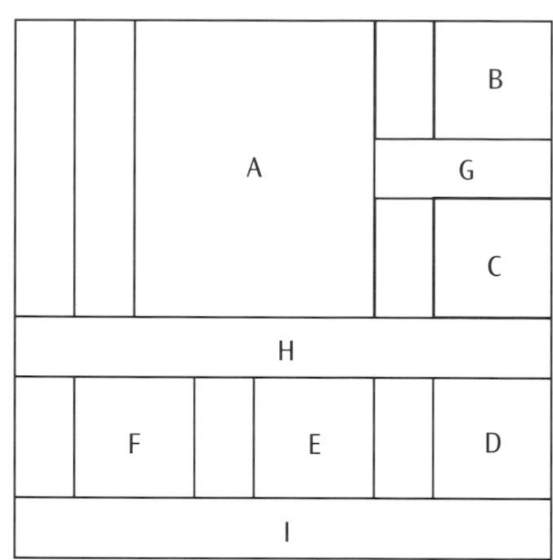

Diagram 1

1. Place blocks A through F on the grid in alphabetical order; refer to Diagram 1. There is a 2" space between the blocks. Place single-fold strips G, H, and I on the grid. Make sure the folded edge of each strip overlaps the raw edge of each block by ¼". Refer to Diagram 1.

2. Make four green folded roses and two pink/floral envelope roses. Place two folded roses and one envelope rose in each bottom corner of block A, beneath the edge of strip H.

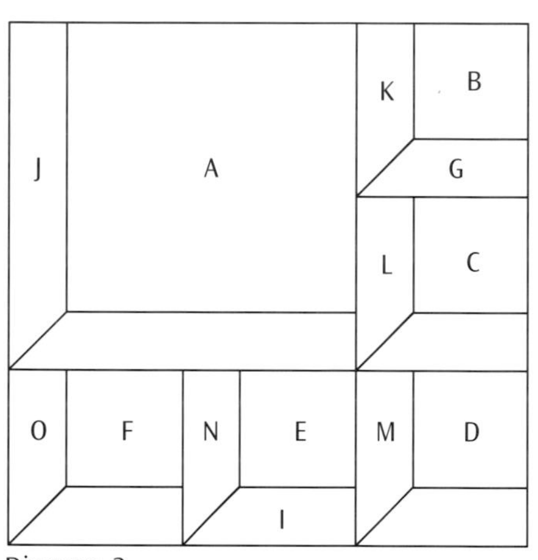

Diagram 2

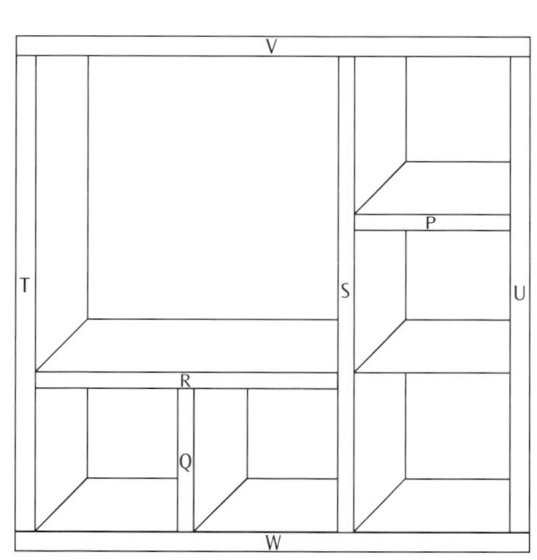

Diagram 3

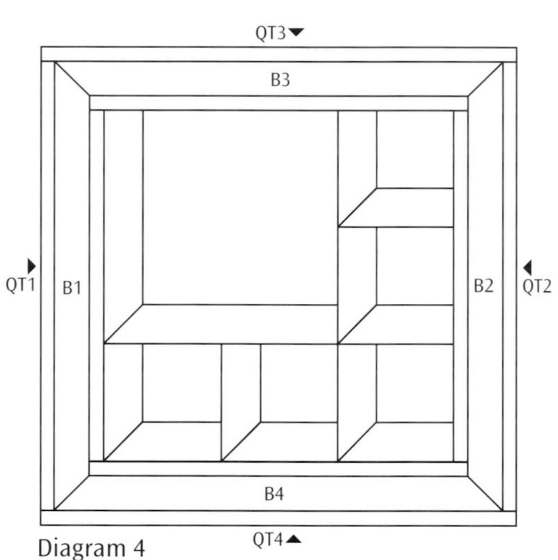

Diagram 4

3. Place the folded edge of miter-fold strips J, K, L, M, N and O onto the grid; overlap the raw edges of the blocks by ¼". Fold under the corner of each miter-fold strip; press in the miter. Trim out the excess fabric under the fold. If desired, use extra spray adhesive or a fabric glue stick to help hold the strips down. Refer to Diagram 2 for placement.

4. Add double-fold strips P and Q; these are your shortest strips. Both edges of each double-fold strip are finished. Cover the raw edges of the blocks when you place the double-fold strips, and cut the strips to fit as you go. Add the remaining strips in alphabetical order. Refer to Diagram 3.

5. Place the border strips on the quilt according to their numbered order. Start with B1, then add B2, B3 and B4. Refer to Diagram 4.

6. Extend each border strip to the final edge of the grid. Overlap B3 on the corners of B1 and B2. Fold the edge under at a 45-degree angle, and press in a miter on both ends. Repeat for B4 over B1 and B2.

Stitch

1. Replace the presser foot on the sewing machine with a walking foot. Use a zigzag stitch or any other decorative stitch that works with the walking foot to stitch down all of the vertical seams in the quilt to anchor all of the pieces together and quilt through the batting and backing fabric with one stitch.

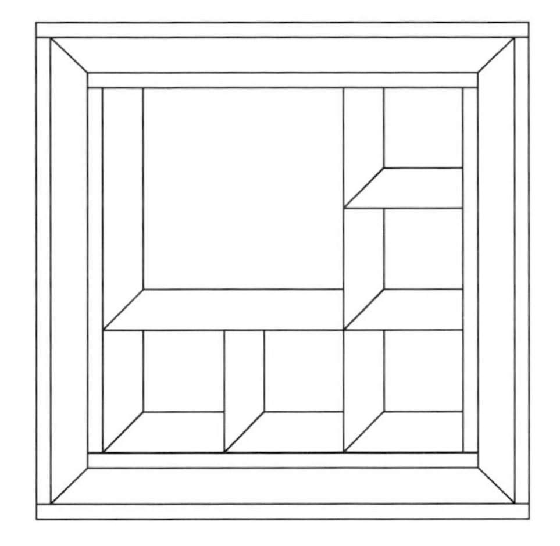

2. Remove the paper tape from the quick-turn strips. Overlap the edge of each quick-turn strip by ½" over the side border of the quilt. Make two pink envelope roses, and slip one rose in each corner of the quilt beneath the quick-turn strip. Steam press the strip to hold it in place; press from both sides of the quilt.

3. Stitch down the quick-turn strip to the edge of the quilt. Trim the ends even with the top and bottom edges of the quilt.

4. Repeat Steps 2 and 3 for the opposite side of the quilt.

5. Overlap by ½" the edge of the quick-turn strip over the top border of the quilt. Press the strip up to 6" from each corner; press the strip from both sides of the quilt.

6. Extend the ends of strip 1" to 2" past the quilt edge. Fold the ends of the strip up, right sides together. Pin the edges together.

7. For the straight corners, begin stitching in the middle of the strip, and backstitch to the edge. Continue stitching again to the top of the strip; backstitch and cut the threads. Avoid catching the edge of the quilt when stitching.

8. Trim the corner. Turn the quick-turn strip back to cover the unfinished edge of the quilt. Stitch down the strip to the edge of the quilt.

9. Repeat Steps 5 through 8 for the bottom of the quilt.

Frog Pond Baby Quilt

Finished Size: 34" x 40"

Round out the nursery with this sew-simple baby quilt. Bright fabrics make the quilt fun, while blooming bias strips add a cuddly embellishment that baby will love to touch.

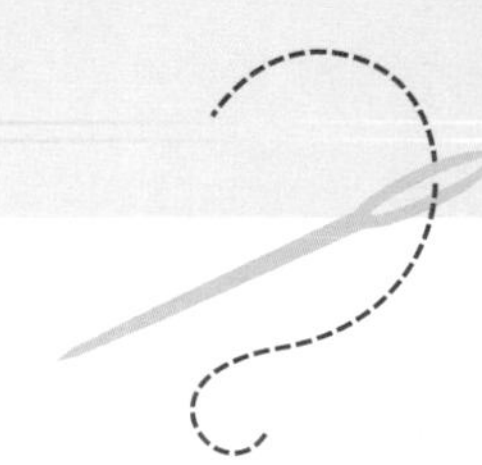

Materials

- 1 yd. frog pond border print, or other theme print with the border printed parallel to the selvedge (border strips)
- 1 yd. small-scale floral or contrasting print (2" strips)
- 1 yd. large-scale butterfly print or other theme print to coordinate with the border print (center strip)
- 1¼ yd. pastel bright square or geometric print to coordinate with other fabrics (backing, first border, 2" strips)
- 3 yd. chenille bias strip trim or other embellishment, such as chenille rickrack
- 1 yd. cotton batting
- 1 package fusible quilt top grid
- Thread to match the backing fabric
- Sewing tools and supplies

NOTE: All strips for this project are cut lengthwise on the grain.

From	Cut	For
Border print	2 strips, 7" x 36"	Edge of quilt top
Small-scale floral	2 strips, 4" x 36"	Double-fold strips
Butterfly print	1 strip, 11" x 36"	Center of quilt top
Geometric print	1 rectangle, 38½" x 44½" 2 strips, 4½" x 36"	Backing and border Single-fold strips
Fusible quilt top grid	1 rectangle, 34" x 40"	Quilt top grid
Batting	1 rectangle, 34" x 40"	Batting

Layer

1. Prepare the single-fold and double-fold strips. For detailed instructions, refer to One Stitch Basics in Part 1.

2. Use a dry iron on a medium setting to fuse the quilt top grid to the batting.

3. Fold the backing fabric in half vertically, then horizontally. Press the creases. Unfold the backing fabric, and lay it out wrong side up. Spray the wrong side of the backing fabric with temporary spray adhesive to make it tacky.

4. Fold the grid/batting sandwich in half vertically, then horizontally; crease the sandwich. Center the grid/batting sandwich with the grid side up on the backing fabric; an equal amount of backing should show all the way around the grid/batting. Smooth the grid/batting sandwich in place, and secure it to the backing fabric. Spray the grid with temporary spray adhesive to make it tacky.

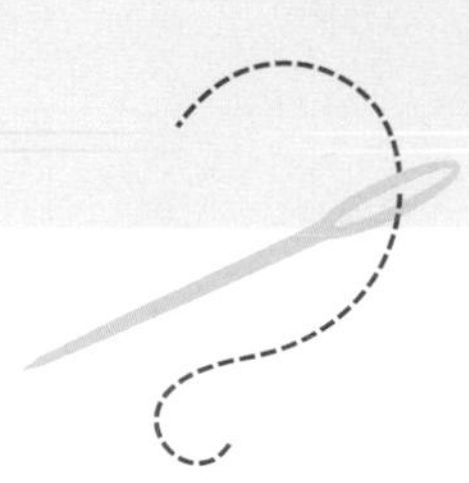

Arrange

1. Starting in the center of the grid, place the 11" butterfly print strip right side up on the grid.

2. Place the folded edge of the single-fold strip on one side of the 11" strip; overlap the strips by ½". Repeat for the other side of the center strip. The finished size of the center theme strip is 10".

3. Lay one double-fold strip next to the single-fold strip. Overlap the raw edge of the single-fold strip by ½".

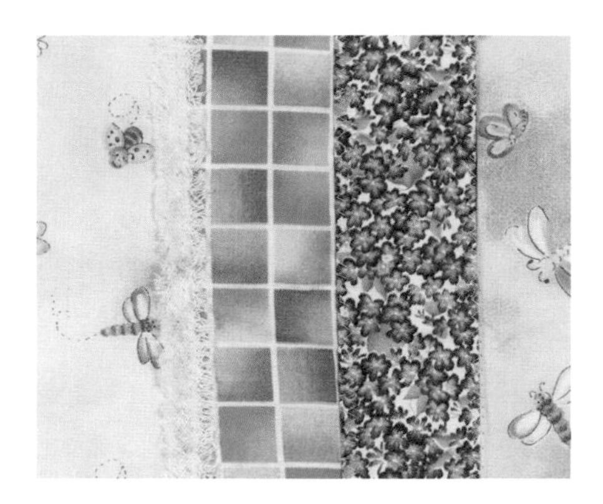

◀ 4. Place a chenille bias strip or other trim between the two narrow strips on both sides of the quilt to create contrast and interest.

5. Lay the border print next to the double-fold strip. Place the raw edge ½" under the double-fold strip. The border will cover the remaining outside raw edges of the strips; the finished size of the border print strip is 6".

6. Fold the edges of the border fabric to create a border fold finish. For detailed instructions, refer to One Stitch Basics in Part 1. Pin the edges in place.

Stitch

1. Replace the sewing machine's presser foot with a walking foot. Starting in the center of the panel, outline any of the motifs you want to stand out. Once you complete the center of the panel begin stitching on the first border. Proceed out from the center of the quilt stitching in the following order: side, side, top and bottom.

2. Use a large zigzag or blanket stitch to stitch down the folded border edge; be sure to catch the raw edges of the fabric strips.

Quick and Cuddly Fleece Quilt

Finished Size: 41" x 51"

This cozy fleece quilt is sure to become a crowd-pleaser with the blanket-toting toddlers in your life. Easy-care fleece offers opportunities for several shortcuts. Because fleece doesn't ravel, there's no extra hemming, folding or finishing needed. And, the thick fleece does double duty as a backing fabric and batting; just be careful when you choose your fabrics so the fleece pattern doesn't cause shadowing behind the printed center panel.

Materials

- 1 printed fabric panel
- 1½ yd. coordinating fleece, 58/60" wide
- 12 wt. thread to match the fleece
- Clear acrylic ruler with scalloped edge
- 18mm or 28mm rotary cutter
- Sewing tools and supplies

NOTE: Solid fleece will give you more flexibility in your quilt design and will allow you create a quilt up to 58" wide by any length desired. Some designs, like the Bubble Buddy fleece, only can be used if the width of the fleece (60") is actually used as the length of the quilt. To figure out how to work around a printed fleece motif, subtract the length of the fabric panel (42") from the fleece width (60"). Divide the remainder (18") by 2 to figure out how much fabric is on either end of the quilt (9"); the single-fold border will be half of that amount (4½"), all the way around the quilt. Add the remainder (18") to the width of the panel (34") to figure out the cut size of the length of the fleece (52").

From	Cut	For
Printed fabric panel	1 rectangle, 34" x 42"	Quilt top
Fleece	1 rectangle, 52" x 60"	Backing and border

Layer and Arrange

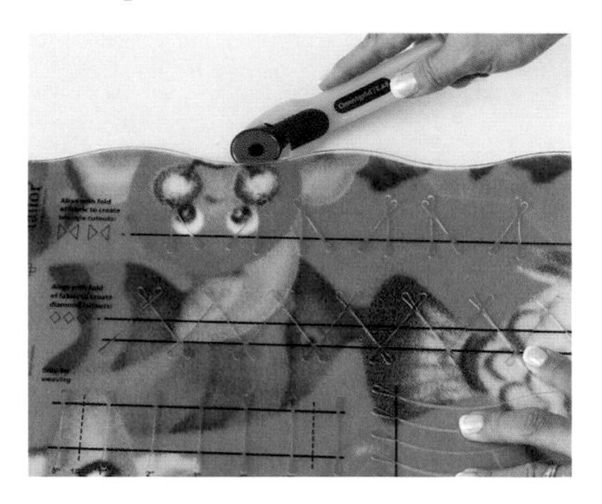

◀ 1. Place the scalloped edge of the ruler against the outside edge of the fleece. Use an 18mm or 28mm rotary cutter, which easily fits into the ruler's curves, to cut the edges along the fleece.

2. Fold the printed fabric panel in half horizontally, then vertically, to find the center. Put a safety pin in the center to mark the spot. Press the pinned fabric panel to remove any creases; you won't be able to press it after the fabric and fleece are sewn together.

3. Fold the fleece into quarters to find the center. Use a safety pin to mark the center. Avoid pressing the fleece, because it will destroy the nap of the fabric.

4. Center the fabric panel over the fleece fabric; match the safety pins.

5. On the short sides of the quilt, fold the fleece up to and over the raw edge of the fabric panel; overlap the fabric by ½". Pin.

◀ 6. On the long sides of the quilt, fold the fleece up to and over the raw edge of the fabric panel; overlap by ½". Pin.

7. Use No. 2 safety pins to pin through the center of the fabric panel, into the fleece. This will prevent stretching during the quilting process.

Stitch

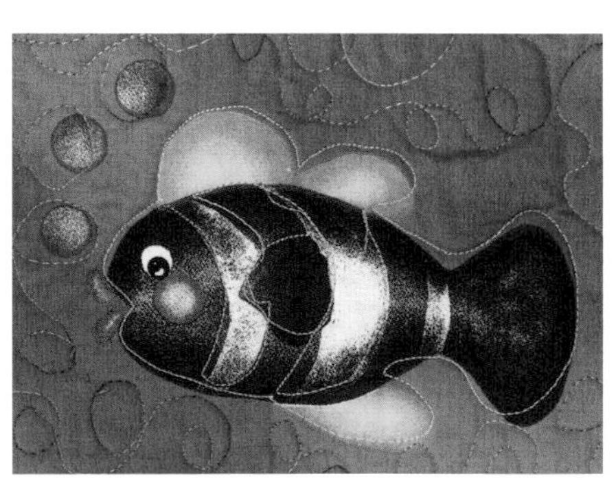

◀ 1. Replace the sewing machine's presser foot with a walking foot. Starting in the center of the panel, outline any of the motifs you want to stand out. Once you complete the center of the panel, stitch on the first border and proceed out from the center of the quilt to stitch the sides, the top and the bottom.

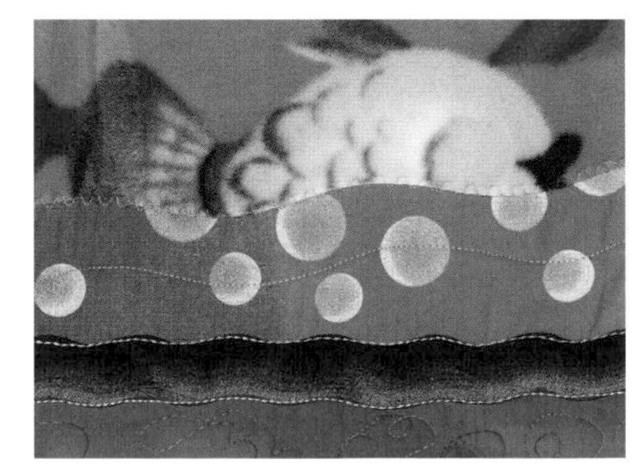

2. Use a large zigzag or blanket stitch to stitch down the folded fleece edge; be sure to catch the raw edge of the fabric panel.

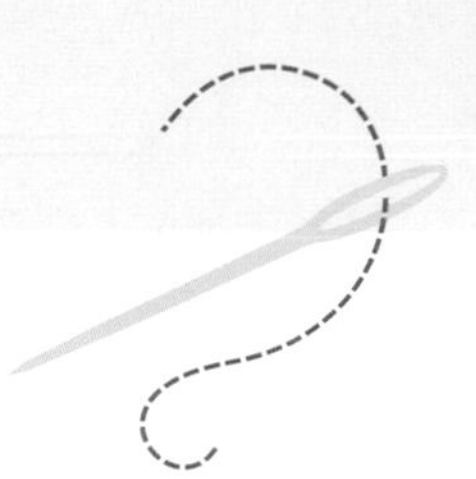

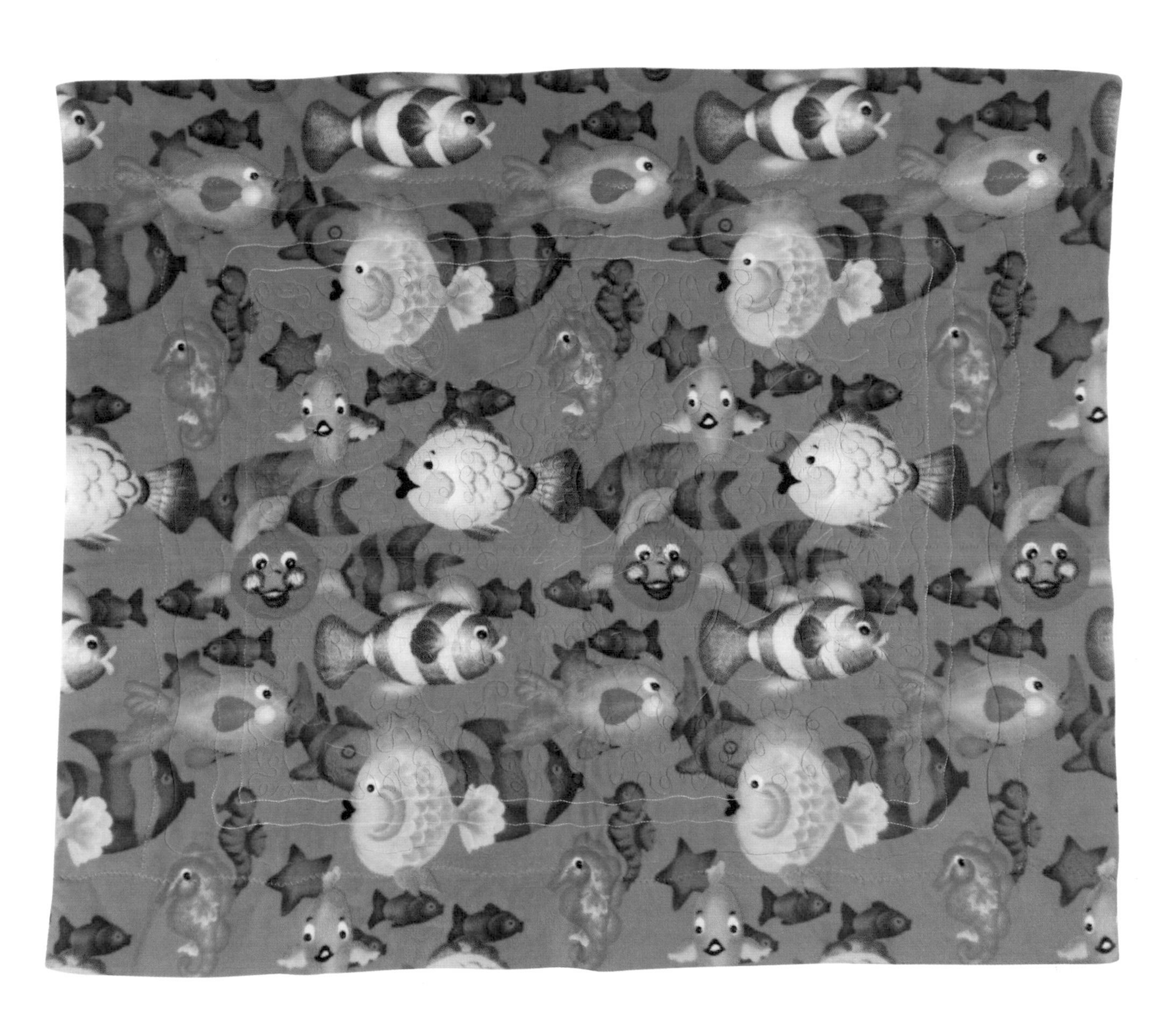

One Stitch Sampler Quilt

Finished Size: 31" x 31"

Master the basics of several One Stitch techniques in one sitting with this sampler quilt. This four-pane quilt project showcases several staples of One Stitch quilting: appliqué, fabric folding, crazy patchwork, One Stitch strips and finishing techniques.

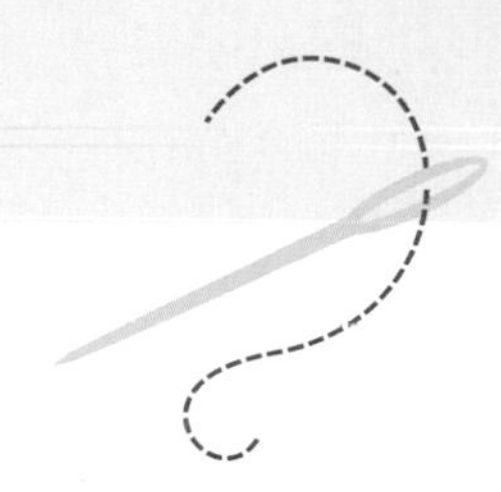

Materials

- 2 yd. violet fern print (backing, borders, applique, crazy patch, star block)
- 1¼ yd. purple crackle or tonal print (borders; crazy patch, and star blocks, flower appliqué)
- 1 yd. green sponge or batik print (block background, crazy patch)
- ½ yd. pink crackle or tonal print (sashing, star block, crazy patch)
- ½ yd. grass green crackle or tonal print (borders, star)
- ½ yd. hunter green crackle or tonal print (crazy patch, leaves)
- ⅓ yd. violet small-scale floral print (crazy patch, flower appliqué)
- 1 Pansy block from the Garden Path Art to Sew collection, or other large-scale floral print (cutout block)
- 1 yd. batting
- 1 package fusible quilt top grid
- Fusible tape, ½" and ⅝" wide
- Thread to complement the fabrics
- Crazy Patch Purse patterns on pages 120 and 121, and One Stitch Sampler Flower Appliqué pattern on page 122
- Sewing tools and supplies

From	Cut	For
Purple crackle	4 strips, 7½" x 42" 10 squares, 3" x 3" 1 square, 10" x 10" 1 Background Petal Unit using Flower Appliqué pattern	Quick-turn, double-load strips for outer border Nine-patch star Crazy patch Appliqué flower
Violet fern	1 square, 32" x 32" 4 strips, 1½" x 42" 3 squares, 3" x 3" 1 square, 10" x 10" 1 each of Petal 1, 2, 3, 4 and 5 using Flower Appliqué pattern	Backing Miter-fold strips for border Nine-patch star Crazy patch Appliqué flower
Grass green crackle	4 strips, 2½" x 42" 1 square, 3" x 3" 1 square, 10" x 10"	Single-fold strips for border Nine-patch star Crazy patch
Pink crackle	2 strips, 2½" x 42" 2 strips, 2" x 42" 1 square, 3" x 3" 1 square, 10" x 10"	Single-fold strips for sashing Double-fold strips for sashing Nine-patch star Crazy patch
Hunter green crackle	1 square, 10" x 10" 1each of Stem and Leaf 1, 2 and 3 using Flower Appliqué pattern	Crazy patch Appliqué flower Appliqué flower Appliqué flower Appliqué flower
Violet floral	1 square, 10" x 10" 1 each of Bud 1, 2 and 3 using Flower Appliqué pattern	Crazy patch Appliqué flower
Green sponge	4 squares, 10" x 10" 1 rectangle, 10" x 18"	Background squares Crazy patch
Art to Sew block/floral	Fussy cut one motif to fit within a 10" x 10" square	Cutout patch
Fusible quilt top grid	1 square, 30" x 30"	Quilt top grid
Batting	1 square, 30" x 30" 4 strips, 3½" x 42" 4 strips, 3" x 42"	Batting Quick-turn, double-load strips for outer border Quick-turn, double-load strips for outer border

Layer

1. Prepare the single-fold, double-fold and miter-fold strips. For detailed instructions, refer to One Stitch Basics in Part 1.

2. Use a dry iron on a medium setting to fuse the quilt top grid to the batting. Cut the grid/batting sandwich down to 28" x 28".

3. Fold the backing fabric in half vertically, then horizontally. Press the creases. Unfold the backing fabric, and lay it out wrong side up. Spray the wrong side of the backing fabric with temporary spray adhesive to make it tacky.

4. Fold the grid/batting sandwich in half vertically, then horizontally; crease the sandwich. Center the grid/batting sandwich with the grid side up on the backing fabric; an equal amount of backing should show all the way around the grid/batting. Smooth the grid/batting sandwich in place, and secure it to the backing fabric. Spray the grid with temporary spray adhesive.

Arrange

1. Make the nine-patch star, crazy patch, appliqué and cutout blocks. For detailed instructions, refer to One Stitch Basics in Part 1.

2. Count in four squares from the left-hand corner of the quilt top grid. Place the first of the four blocks on the grid.

3. Add the remaining blocks to create a layout of two blocks across and two blocks down. The raw edges of the blocks should butt up against each other, but they shouldn't overlap. The double-fold sashing strips will cover the raw edges.

4. Once you are satisfied with the position of each block, place a piece of ⅝"-wide fusible tape under each corner of each block. Press the blocks to hold them in place.

5. Press a strip of ½"-wide fusible tape to the wrong side of the sashing strips. Place the double-fold sashing strips between the blocks in a plus-sign configuration. The sashing strip will overlap the blocks by ½". Cut the sashing strips even with the outside edges of the blocks.

6. Place a single-fold sashing strip at the outside edge of the top of the blocks so the folded edge of each strip is against each block's raw edges; spray temporary spray adhesive to the inside of each strip to hold it together. Add the bottom strip, then the side strips. Cut the strips to fit. Once each strip is in place, apply fusible tape to hold it.

7. Add the grass green single-fold strips for the next border, starting with the top, then adding the bottom and side borders. Refer to One Stitch Basics in Part 1 for detailed instructions. Remember to secure the strips once they are placed to your satisfaction.

8. Add the violet fern miter-fold border to the quilt; refer to One Stitch Basics in Part 1 for detailed instructions.

9. Press all of the strips and blocks to the fusible quilt top grid to secure them. Pin baste the sampler using No. 2. safety pins; this will help prevent shifting. Avoid pinning across any seam lines, such as along the edges of borders.

Stitch

1. Free-motion quilt the block backgrounds or motifs as desired.

2. Set the sewing machine to sew a medium zigzag stitch with a length of 2.5 and a width of 3.5. Stitch down through all of the patches; form the vertical lines first, then follow with the horizontal lines. Finish by following the diagonal lines of the triangles in the nine-patch star and the edges of the cutout motif.

3. Stitch down the folded edge of the borders and ¼" from the outside edges of the quilt.

4. Trim the batting and grid even with the last border.

5. Stitch around the final border.

6. Add the quick-turn, double-load strips, and complete the rounded-edge corners. For detailed instructions, refer to One Stitch Basics in Part 1.

Patterns

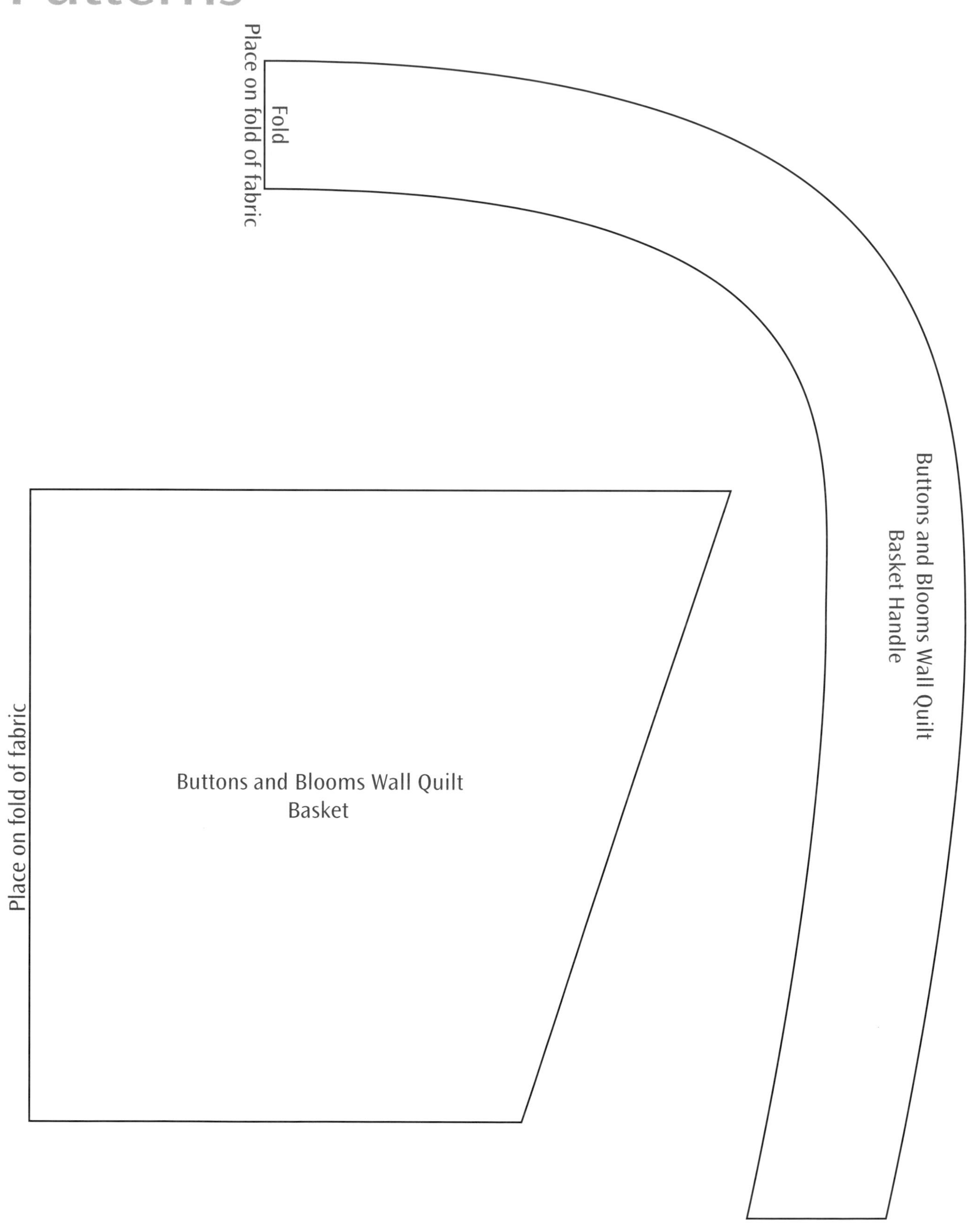

Place on fold of fabric
Fold
Buttons and Blooms Wall Quilt
Basket Handle
Place on fold of fabric
Buttons and Blooms Wall Quilt
Basket

Chasing Butterflies Wall Hanging

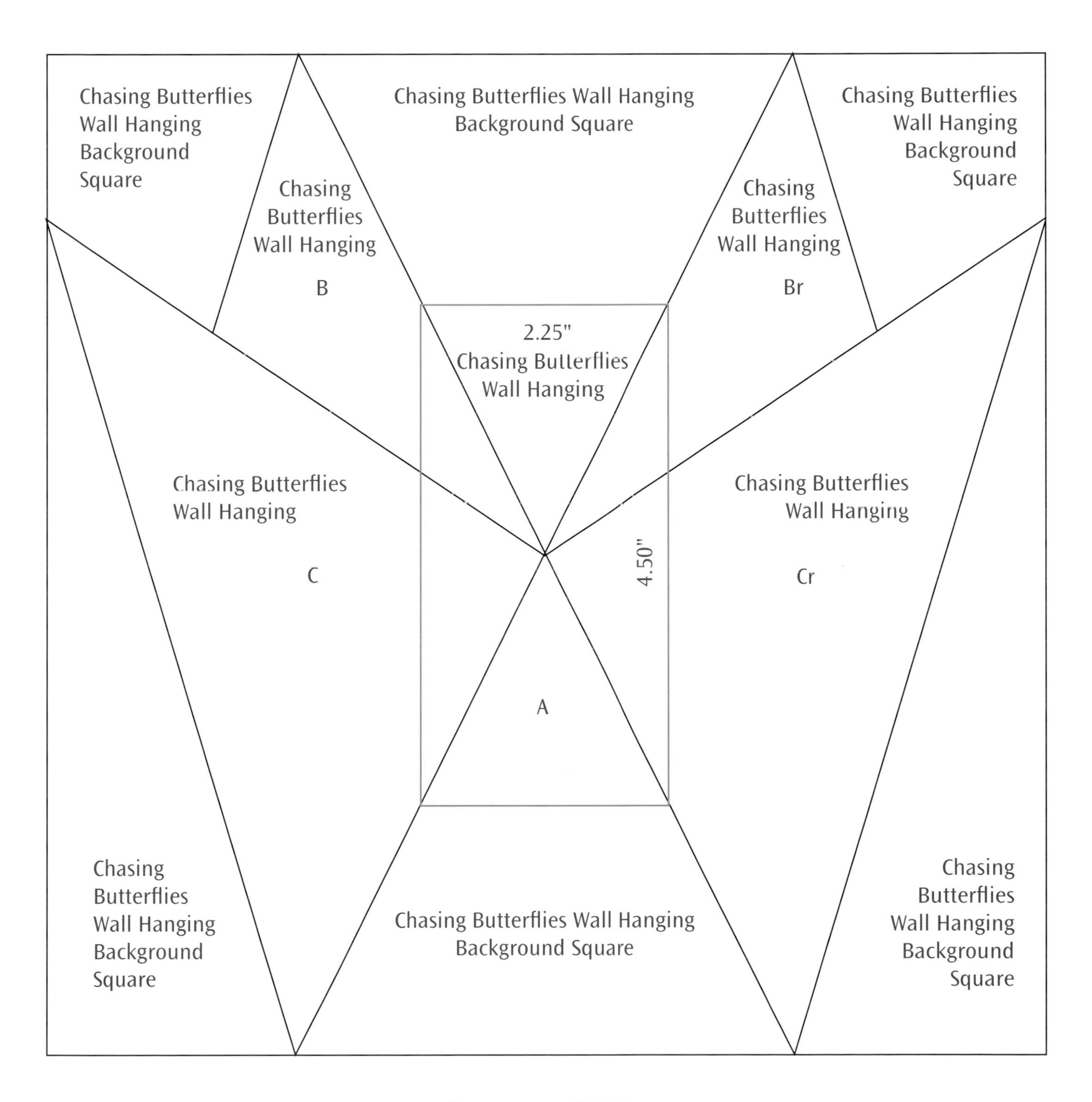

Increase 20%

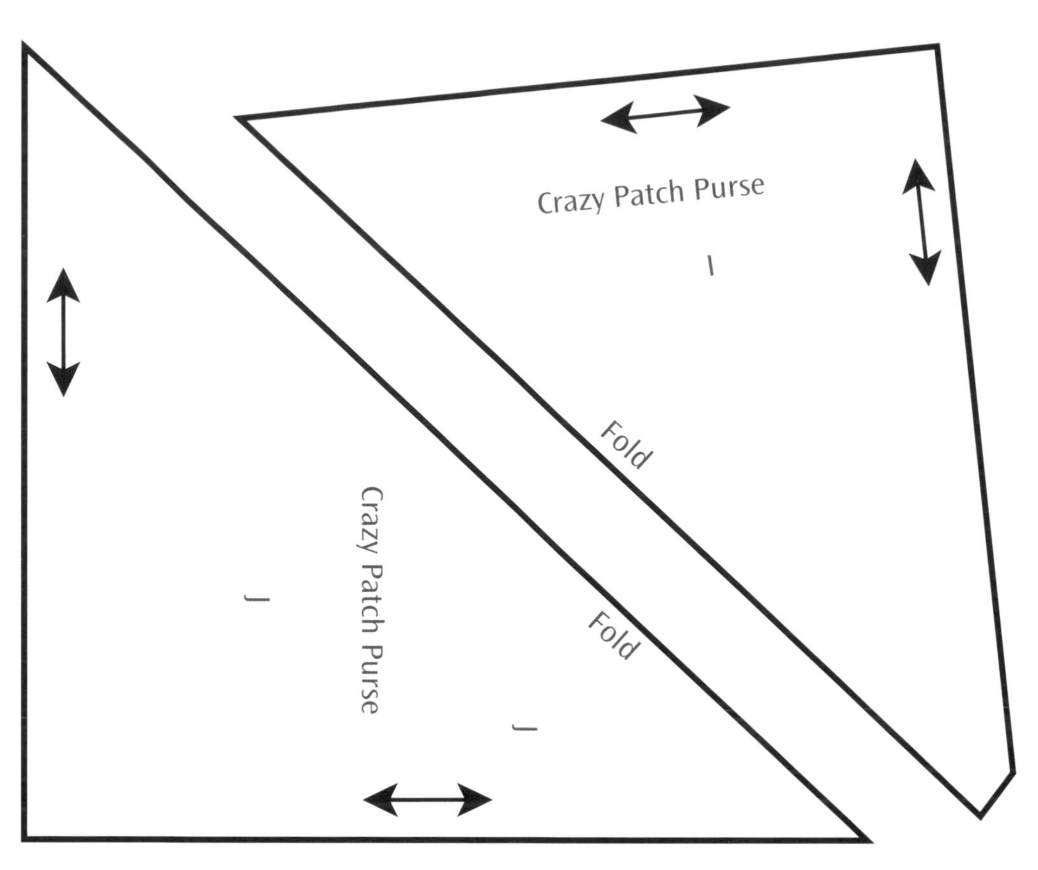

Crazy Patch Purse

F_2

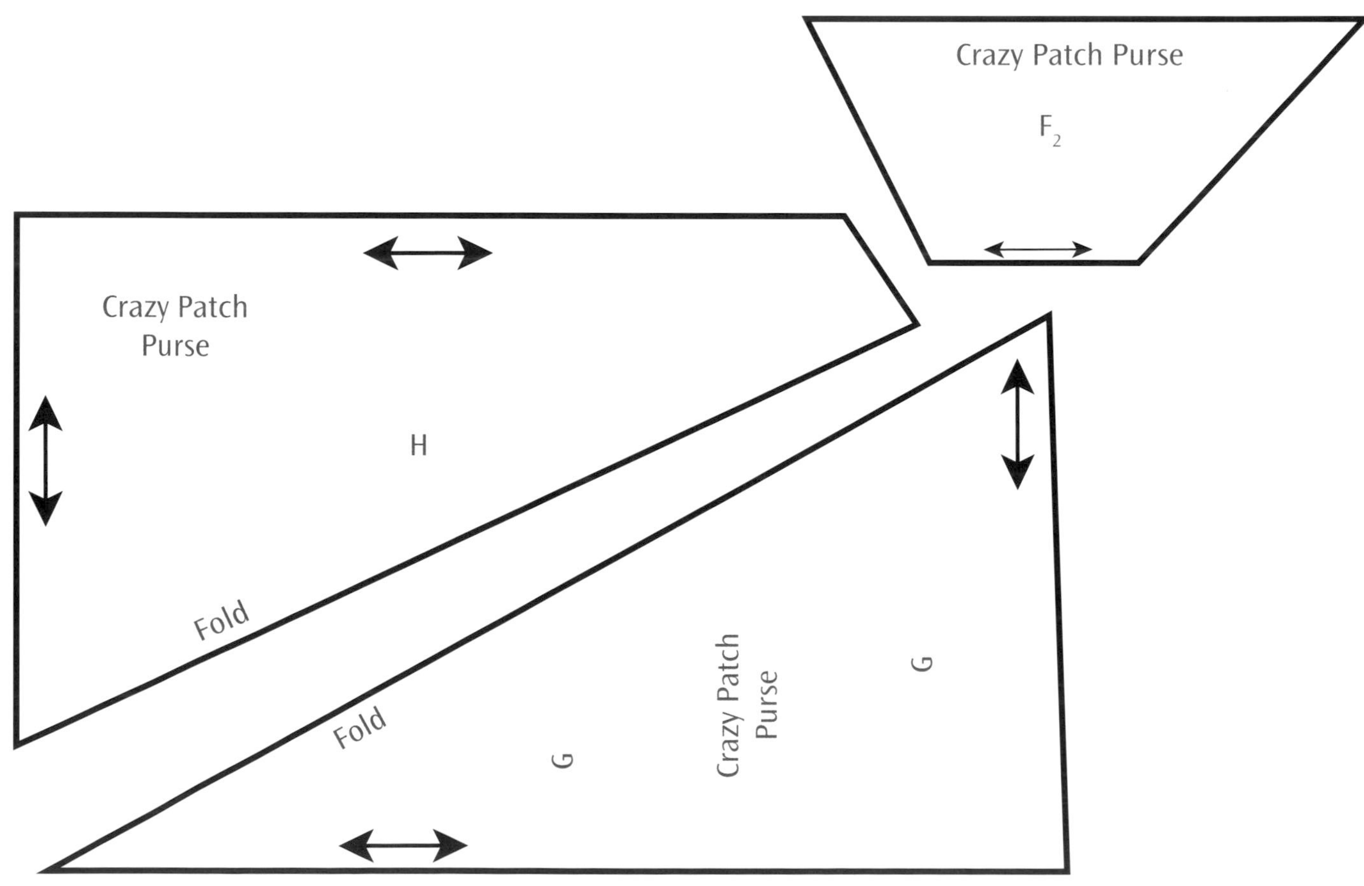

Increase all 20%

Crazy Patch Purse

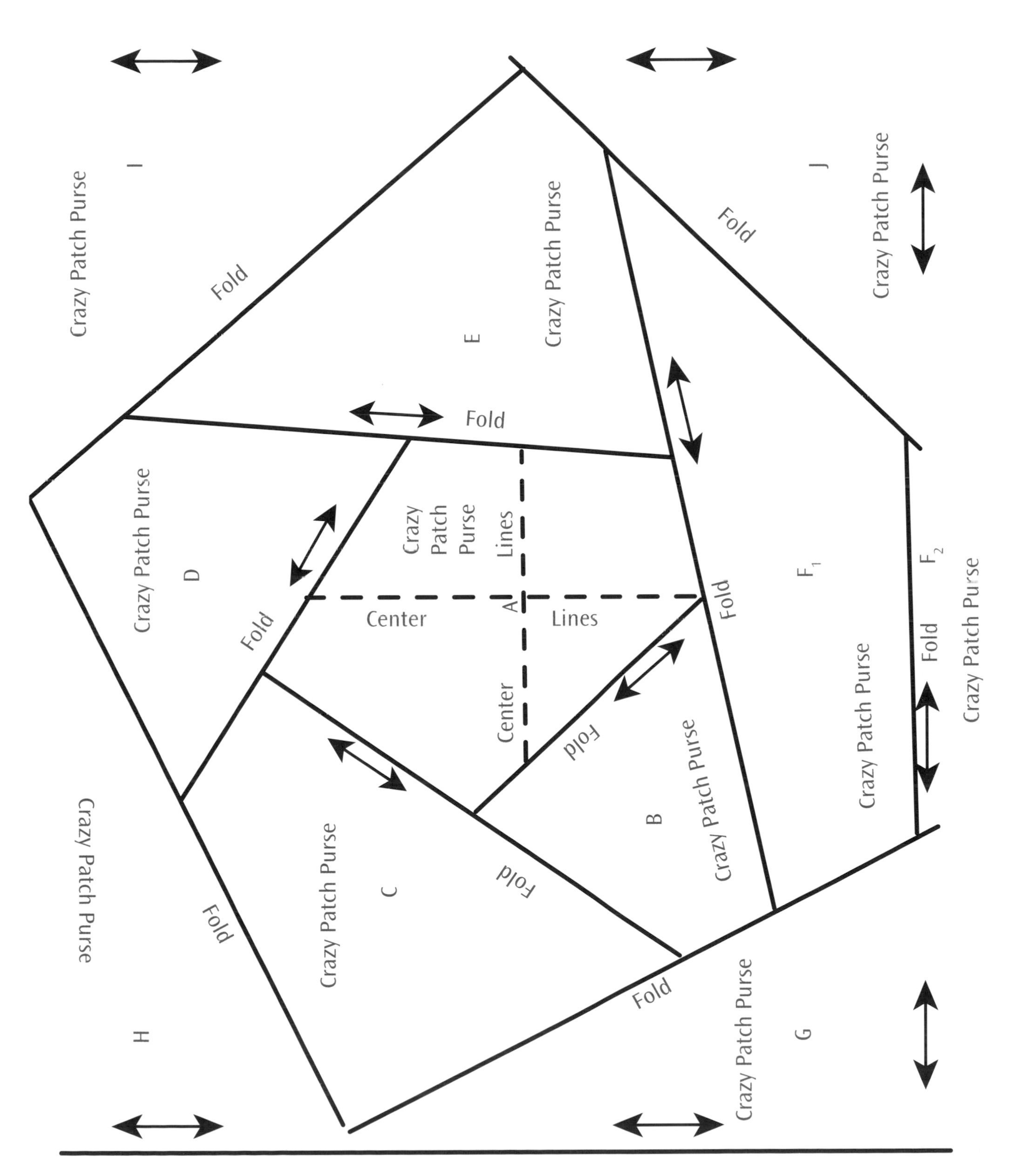

Increase 20%

One Stitch Sampler Flower Appliqué

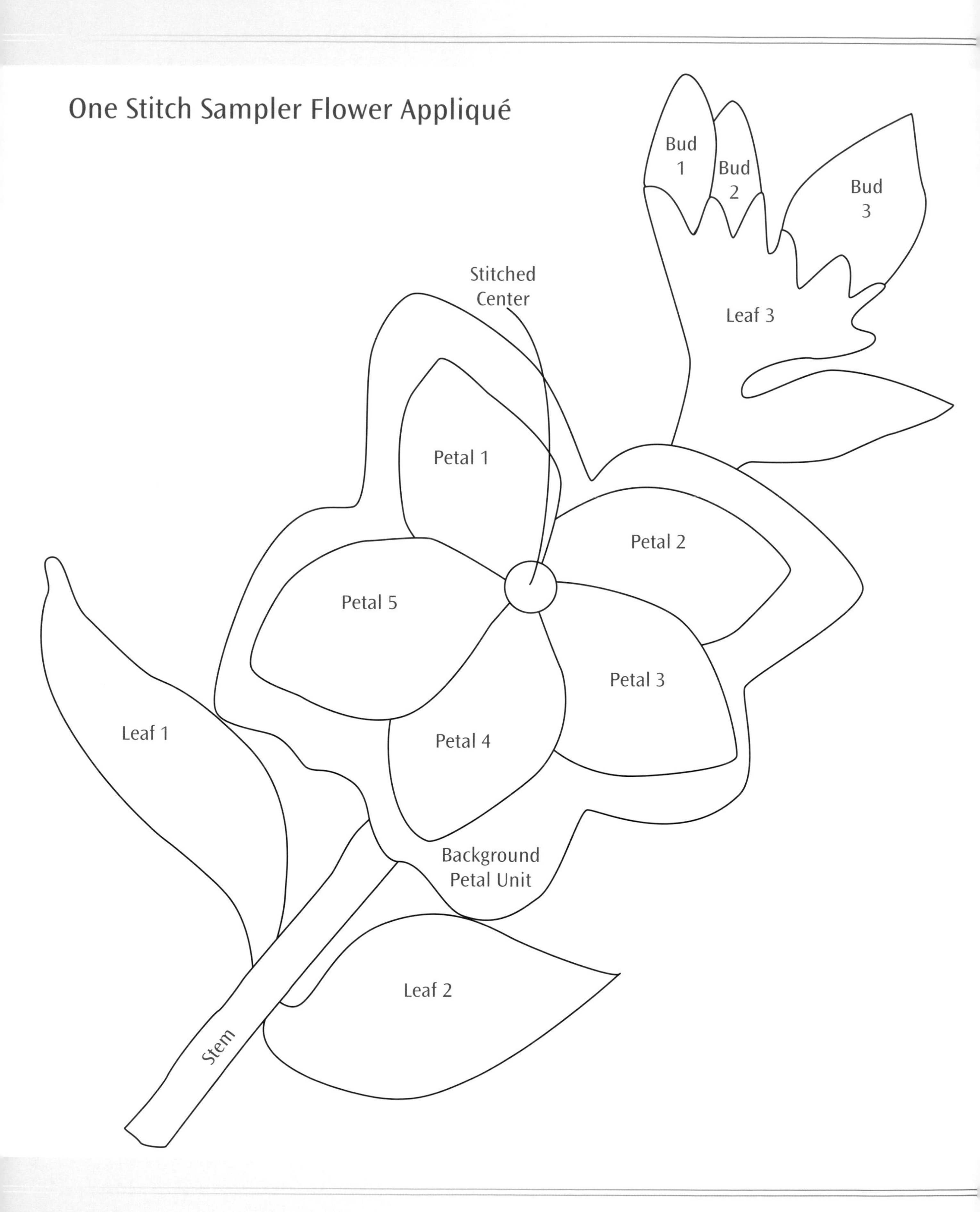

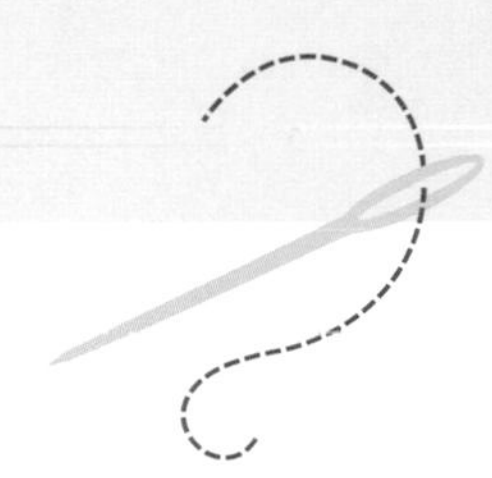

Glossary

APPLIQUÉ — A technique where small pieces of fabric are sewn or fused to a background fabric to form designs. Appliqué can be done by hand, by machine or by using fusible web. It also may be combined with pieced blocks. The One Stitch method uses a fusible web style of appliqué. For more information, refer to Parts 1 and 2.

ART TO SEW — A line of fabric produced by Springs Creative Products Group that features reproductions of Donna Dewberry's artwork and coordinating prints. The 200 thread count, 100 percent cotton fabric is sold in small and large blocks, with coordinating prints sold by the yard.

BACKGROUND FABRIC — The fabric used as the foundation block upon which appliqué and/or patchwork pieces are fused via the One Stitch method. The background fabric also may be referred to as a background square. For more information, refer to Part 1.

BACKING — The fabric on the back side of a quilt. The backing fabric is the third of three layers in a One Stitch quilt sandwich, with the quilt top on the top, the batting in the middle and the backing on the bottom. The One Stitch method also uses the backing layer as the final border in certain finishing methods.

BASTING — The One Stitch method of securing the three layers of a quilt sandwich that utilizes No. 2 safety pins or a basting spray adhesive. We prefer quilting safety pins by Dritz and KK 2000 temporary spray adhesive. For more information, refer to Part 1.

BATTING — The middle layer of a quilt sandwich. The batting is between the quilt top and the backing. We prefer Warm & White 100 percent cotton batting, as it lays flat and can be cut with a rotary cutter the same way fabric can. For more information, refer to Part 1.

BIAS — The diagonal direction across the surface of a woven fabric. The bias is at a 45-degree angle to the lines of the warp and weft. Fabric cut on the bias stretches and must be handled with care.

BINDING — The straight-of-grain or bias strips of fabric that often are folded double and used to cover the raw edges and batting of a quilt. The One Stitch method uses the backing fabric to create the binding on smaller-size quilts. A straight-of-grain strip binding is used to cover the final raw edge of all quilts that have a finished width larger than the backing fabric. For more information, refer to Part 1.

BORDER — A strip of fabric or pieced strip of fabric that is joined to the edges of the inner quilt and used to frame it. The One Stitch method uses double-fold strips that overlap the inner quilt's raw edges to provide the frame. For more information, refer to Part 1.

BORDER-FOLD HANGING SLEEVE — A hanging sleeve that is formed when backing fabric is brought over to the front of the quilt, but the corners aren't sewn shut. The resulting pocket allows you to insert a simple dowel rod to hang a quilt. For more information, refer to Part 1.

CLIPPED CORNERS — Folding down the corners of the last border strip to create a triangle, then pressing a crease line and cutting or clipping the corners on the crease.

CUTOUTS — A One Stitch method from an old style of appliqué also known as broderie perse. The cutouts technique calls for the quilter to cut out images from a printed fabric, then use a pressure-sensitive interfacing to fuse it to a new background fabric. For more information, refer to Part 1.

DENSITY — How close design elements are placed on a fabric design. Fabrics that are printed with the design elements that are very close together tend to blend into one another, which causes the viewer to see an allover color and shape instead of the actual printed design. Fabrics that are printed with a large amount of space around the design elements tend to retain their overall design and be viewed as containing separate colors.

DOUBLE-FOLD BORDER FINISH — The One Stitch finishing technique that uses the backing fabric to form the final border and finished edge of a quilt. For more information, refer to Part 1.

DOUBLE-FOLD STRIP — A strip used in One Stitch quilting, most often for sashing between blocks. To create a double-fold strip, cut a strip of fabric twice the width of the finished measurement. Fold the strip in half lengthwise, placing the fabric wrong sides together. Open the strip and refold it to bring both raw edges toward the crease line in the middle; this will leave two folded edges on the long sides of the strip to form the double-fold strip. For more information, refer to Part 1.

DOUBLE-LOAD STRIP —A quick-turn strip that is loaded with two strips of batting. This strip primarily is used in the One Stitch method to add borders to larger quilts. For more information, refer to Part 1.

Fat Quarter — A cut of fabric that measures 18" x 22". A fat quarter contains the same overall surface area as a standard quarter yard of fabric that measures 9" x 44", but the fat quarter offers greater versatility to quilters because it can accommodate larger blocks.

Feed Dogs — Mechanical teeth that move to pull fabric through a sewing machine. The feed dogs are located beneath the presser foot.

Finger Pressing — A method to form temporary creases for appliqué turned edges or seam allowances. Fold the fabric, then run a fingernail along the fold to make it flat. You also can use a wooden finger-pressing tool or bamboo skewer to help you make creases.

Folded Rosebuds — Squares that are folded in half and folded again on the diagonal to form a three-dimensional triangle. You can make the first fold in half on the diagonal or the second fold in half on the diagonal. This way, you end up with either a square or a rectangle. Both methods are useful, depending on the project. For more information, refer to Part 1.

Finished Size — The final sewn measurement or dimensions of a completed block without seam allowances. The One Stitch method requires a 1" seam allowance to be added to the finished size of the patchwork or appliquéd block; thus, a finished 6" block would be cut 7" to allow for ¼" seam allowances and joining strips.

Fusion — The eye's ability to blend two or more colors on a densely printed multicolored fabric. A print that is densely printed with two or more colors will look different in the overall project than when it was selected from the bolt. A good rule of thumb to practice when buying and selecting fabrics is to view them from a distance of at least 5 feet. This way, your eyes will be able to adjust to see the true colors and degree of contrast in the fabrics.

Fusible — Any web, tape or interfacing that can be ironed onto a fabric. Fusibles can be used to support fabrics or to make appliqué faster and easier. Fusible webs, tapes and interfacing play a key role in the One Stitch method of quilting. For more information, refer to Part 1.

Fussy Cut — Precisely cutting out specific areas of fabric to use an image or motif, particularly for appliqué.

Grain — The lengthwise and crosswise threads, also known as warp and weft, of a woven fabric. Determine the grain of any fabric by tugging on the edge. The lengthwise grains will make a snapping sound but won't stretch or give. Crosswise grains will make a thudding sound when pulled, but they will have stretch and give.

Grid — Fusible interfacing that is marked into equal segments, usually 1" to 2". Grid is used in the One Stitch method to create seamless quilts. For more information, refer to Part 1.

Hanging Sleeve — A tube or sleeve typically sewn on the backside of a quilt at the top of the piece to allow it to be hung or displayed. The One Stitch method allows you to create an instant hanging sleeve by using the Border-Fold Hanging Sleeve technique to bring the backing around to the front of the quilt. For more information, refer to Part 1.

Intensity — The purity or strength of a color or fabric compared with the color wheel. Utilizing some fabrics that contain a high saturation of pure hue or color can add a lot of excitement to your quilt. Such fabrics often are referred to as zingers.

Machine Quilting Stitch — A sewing machine stitch that is made through all three layers of a quilt to hold them together. The One Stitch method uses the machine quilting stitch to secure the quilt pieces and/or appliqués, as well as to quilt through the three layers of the quilt sandwich. There are many styles of machine quilting, including freestyle, stippling and loops.

Matching Points — Traditional ¼" piecing that ensures that the corners of blocks or points of stars match at the seam line. The prevents points from being cut off by the seam. The One Stitch method eliminates the need to piece a quilt, and it allows a 1" margin, so no points are cut off.

Miter-Fold Strip —A strip used for a border or corner that is folded at a 45-degree angle. For more information, refer to Part 1.

Mitered Corner — A border or corner whose edges are joined at a 45-degree angle.

Motif — The design element, image or drawing used on a quilt block or for an appliqué. An example is a quilt that uses a heart motif or other theme image.

Napkin Fold — The type of fold used to create the triangular Garden Path Napkins featured in Part 2. Fold an 18" square in half on the diagonal, wrong sides together. Sew ¼" around the raw edges, leaving a roughly 5" section open on one side of the napkin. Turn the napkin right sides out, and use a bamboo stiletto or the end of a seam ripper to push the corners out. Press the piece flat, then topstitch ¼" around the outside edge of the napkin. For more information, refer to Part 2.

PATCH — An individual fabric shape that is joined with other patches to make a quilt block or a one-patch style of quilt. Also known as a piece, a patch may be cut by freehand, by using rotary cutting equipment or by using a template. For more information, refer to Part 1.

PATCHWORK — The basic method of making a quilt by sewing many small pieces of fabric together. The One Stitch method does not involve traditional piecing; instead, patches are fused to a foundation block that is cut 1" larger than the finished patchwork block. For more information, refer to Part 1.

PRESSING — Using an iron to press downward to flatten seams and blocks. Pressing differs from ironing, which can distort blocks or seams. For more information, refer to Part 1.

QUICK-TURN FINISH — A One Stitch finish technique that yields a faux binding. To create a quick-turn finish, place the backing fabric and quilt top right sides together, then stitch with a ¼" seam allowance, leaving a 6" opening at the bottom of the quilt to turn the backing fabric right side out. Turn the piece right side out, and press under the raw edge. Stitch the opening closed, and stitch ¼" inside the outside edge to form a fake binding. For more information, refer to Part 1.

QUICK-TURN FOLD STRIP —A strip used in the One Stitch method. To create a quick-turn fold strip, cut the fabric twice the width of your finished measurement plus 1¼" seam allowance. Fold the strip in half lengthwise, fabric wrong sides together. Open the strip, and turn under ½" on both long raw edges. Press ½" fusible tape on the long edge on the right side of the fabric of each side of your strip; leave the paper in place. Use the tape as your guide to turn under a ½" seam allowance to the wrong side of the fabric; press. For more information, refer to Part 1.

QUILT TOP — The top layer of a quilt that typically includes piecing or other decorative techniques and embellishments, such as appliqué.

QUILTING — In general, the process of making a quilt. Quilting also can refer to the act of stitching fabrics and batting together in lines or other patterns to keep the batting in place and to add texture and dimension to a finished piece.

RAW EDGE — The unsewn edge of a piece of fabric or a quilt block.

RIGHT SIDES TOGETHER — Placing the right sides of two fabric layers on top of each other. The right side of the fabric is the one that features the printed design.

ROTARY CUTTING EQUIPMENT — Rotary cutters, mats and rulers used to quickly and precisely cut fabric. A rotary cutter is a tool with a circular blade that cuts through several layers of fabric at once. Rotary cutters work best when used with clear plastic or acrylic rulers, which help to guide blades, and with cutting mats, which protect work surfaces and preserve blades' sharpness. For more information, refer to Part 1.

ROUNDED-CORNER FINISH — A corner style used in the One Stitch method. Use a small, rounded foam plate to trace a rounded corner on the wrong side of the strip. Stitch on the traced line, then backstitch and stop stitching on the inside of the strip. Avoid catching the edge of the quilt when stitching. Trim the corner and quick-turn strip back to cover unfinished edge of the quilt. For more information, refer to Part 1.

SASHING — The fabric that separates blocks on a quilt. Sashing frames blocks and makes quilts larger.

SATIN STITCH — A slanted, tightly packed stitch often used for outlining and with appliqué. A machine satin stitch is made by using a zigzag stitch set a very tight stitch setting.

SCALE — The size of a patterned design on the fabric. Use a variety of small-, medium- and large-scale patterns in projects to create depth and visual interest.

SEAM ALLOWANCE — The width of fabric remaining to the right of a sewn seam. In quilting the seam allowance traditionally is ¼"; garment sewing typically uses a ⅝" seam allowance.

SECURITY BLANKET — A sample quilt sandwich that uses the same fabric and batting as the project that allows you to test thread color, thread tension, stitch length and stitch width before stitching your project. Make a security blanket for every project, and keep it handy at your sewing machine.

SELVAGE — The outer edge of both sides of a woven fabric where the weft turns to go back across and through the warp. This stiffer, denser woven area typically measures ⅓" to ½" wide. The selvage usually is trimmed off, not sewn into a quilt.

SETTING — The way completed blocks are arranged to form the quilt top.

SINGLE-FOLD BORDER FINISH — A One Stitch finishing technique that uses fleece to form the final border and finished edge of a quilt. For more information, refer to Part 1.

SINGLE-FOLD STRIP — A strip used in One Stitch quilting. To create a single-fold strip, cut strip of fabric twice the width of your finished measurement plus ½" seam allowance. Fold the strip in half lengthwise, wrong sides together, then press. For more information, refer to Part 1.

Stash — The term "my stash" or "a stash" refers to a quilter's collection of fabrics.

Spray Adhesive — A product that is sprayed directly onto fabric or batting to temporarily adhere fabric or batting. Spray adhesive typically is used for basting, appliqué and One Stitch patchwork.

Straight-Corner Finish — A One-Stitch finishing technique where edges of a corner or border meet and join perpendicularly. To create a straight-corner finish, begin stitching in the middle of the strip. Backstitch to the edge, continue stitching again to the top of the strip, backstitch again and cut the threads. Avoid catching the edge of the quilt when stitching. Trim the corner and quick-turn strip back to cover unfinished edge of the quilt.

Style Identification — A system to categorize fabrics based on general traits in pattern styles. Style categories include: florals, vines, leaves, novelties, batiks, marbled prints, geometric patterns, checks, plaids, paislies, pin dots, etc. Fabric styles also vary in scale.

Temperature — The warmth or coolness of a color. Warm colors include reds, oranges and yellows, while cool colors include greens, blues and purples. Use colors to help convey a feeling of warmth or coolness in a project.

Template — A shape cut from template plastic or paper-backed fusible web that is used to make pieces of a pattern for quilt blocks or appliqué.

Texture — The combination of a fabric's pattern and scale of design. Quilts, garments and accessories are more interesting and exciting to look at when the fabrics contrast by the use of different sizes of prints and a variety of designs such as geometrics, florals, checks, stripes, dots, etc.

Trim Strip — Folded fabric, ribbon, piping or lace used to trim a block or quilt. These strips don't take up space on the grid or increase the overall size of the quilt. Trim strips often are caught between two borders or a sashing and a border.

Triple-Fold Strip —A double–fold strip that is folded again, one side over the top of the other, to conceal all raw edges. This strip works well for straps on purses and tote bags.

Value — The lightness or darkness of a given fabric. The value of a fabric is relative to each fabric with which it is combined. True value cannot be determined until all fabrics are grouped together. The degree of contrast and value in the design determines the definition of the design. In most quilts there are dark, medium and light fabrics.

Walking Foot — A special presser foot that is attached to a sewing machine that helps to feed the top layer of a quilt fabric sandwich evenly with the feed dogs that are feeding the bottom fabric.

Contributors and Resources

Contributors

Ackfeld Manufacturing
Manufacturer of handcrafted wire products for the crafting, quilting and gift industries.

P.O. Box 539

Reeds Spring, MO 65737

Phone: (888) 272-3135

Fax: (417) 272-3160

E-mail: admin@ackfeldwire.com

Web: www.ackfeldwire.com

KP Books
Publisher of this and other quality how-to books for sewing and quilting, including "Quilting With Donna Dewberry."

700 E. State St.

Iola, WI 54990-0001

Phone: (888) 457-2873

Web: www.krause.com

Dewberry Designs Inc.
Official source for One Stitch Quilting designs, quilting books, One Stitch certification and online purchase of select products, including Chenille-It Blooming Bias strips, Art to Sew fabrics and quilting books by Donna Dewberry and Cindy Casciato.

355 Citrus Tower Blvd., Suite 104

Clermont, FL 34711

Phone: (800) 536-2627

E-mail: e-mail@onestroke.com

Web: www.onestitchquilting.com

Hansen Brand Source
Sales source for TVs, appliances and home furnishings.

990 W. Fulton St.

Waupaca, WI 54981

Phone: (800) 773-4746

June Tailor
Manufacturer of various sewing- and quilting-related products, including June Tailor's White Colorfast Computer Printer Fabric, Quick Fuse Inkjet Fabric Sheets, Quilt Top Express, Sew Station, Fancy Fleece Ruler and Quilt Basting Spray.

P.O. Box 208

Richfield, WI 53076

Phone: (800) 844-5400

E-mail: customerservice@junetailor.com

Web: www.junetailor.com

Lorie's Little Quilts
Manufacturer of a variety of SOFTouch oak quilt hangers.

241 County Road 120

Carthage, MO 64836

Phone: (888) 419-5618

Web: www.lorieslittlequilts.com

Prym Consumer USA Inc.
Manufacturer of sewing, quilting, cutting and craft-related tools and notions, including: Omnigrid rotary cutters, scissors, acrylic rulers, ergonomic thread snips and cutting mats; Omnigrip nonskid rotary cutting grip; Dritz and Collins marking pens, pencils, erasers, tailor's chalk, basting pins, glass-head pins, sewing/craft glue sticks, Seam Squizzers seam rippers, Stitch Witchery fusible tape and Mary Engelbreit pincushions.

P.O. Box 5028

Spartanburg, SC 29304

Web: www.dritz.com

Quiltescape
Exclusive retreats for quilters coordinated by co-author Cindy Casciato and Drew Casciato.

E-mail: cindy@cindycasciato.com

Web: www.quiltescape.com or www.cindycasciato.com

Rowenta
Manufacturer of steamers and irons.

196 Boston Ave.

Medford, MA 02155

Phone: (781) 396-0600

Web: www.rowenta.com

Springs Creative Products Group
Manufacturer of coordinated home furnishings, bed and bath products, and home sewing and quilting fabrics, including the Art to Sew by Donna Dewberry line of printed panels and coordinating prints.

P.O. Box 10232

Rock Hill, SC 29731

Phone: (800) 234-6688

Web: www.springs.com

Sulky of America Inc.
Manufacturer of threads, stabilizers and spray adhesives, including Blendables threads and KK 2000 Temporary Spray Adhesive.

P.O. Box 494129

Port Charlotte, FL 33949-4129

Phone: (800) 874-4115 (to obtain a mail-order source)

E-mail: info@sulky.com

Web: www.sulky.com

The Warm Company

Manufacturer of batting and fusible products, including Warm & White batting, Lite Steam-A-Seam 2 fusible web and Lite Steam-A-Seam 2 fusible tape.

954 E. Union St.

Seattle, WA 98122

Phone: (800) 234-9276

E-mail: info@warmcompany.com

Web: www.warmcompany.com

White Sewing Machines

Manufacturer of sewing machines and accessories, including the Quilter's Star sewing machine and walking foot featured in the photos in this book.

31000 Viking Parkway

Westlake, OH 44145

Phone: (800) 331-3164

Web: www.whitesewing.com

Additional Resources

Annie's Attic

1 Annie Lane

Big Sandy, TX 75755

Phone: (800) 582-6643

Web: www.anniesattic.com

Clotilde LLC

P.O. Box 7500

Big Sandy, TX 75755-7500

Phone: (800) 772-2891

Web: www.clotilde.com

Connecting Threads

P.O. Box 870760

Vancouver, WA 98687-7760

Phone: (800) 574-6454

Web: www.ConnectingThreads.com

Ghee's

2620 Centenary Blvd. No. 2-250

Shreveport, LA 71104

Phone: (318) 226-1701

E-mail: bags@ghees.com

Web: www.ghees.com

Herrschners, Inc.

2800 Hoover Road

Stevens Point, WI 54492-0001

Phone: (800) 441-0838

Web: www.herrschners.com

Home Sew

P.O. Box 4099

Bethlehem, PA 18018-0099

Phone: (800) 344-4739

Web: www.homesew.com

Keepsake Quilting

Route 25

P.O. Box 1618

Center Harbor, NH 03226-1618

Phone: (800) 438-5464

Web: www.keepsakequilting.com

Nancy's Notions

333 Beichl Ave.

P.O. Box 683

Beaver Dam, WI 53916-0683

Phone: (800) 833-0690

Web: www.nancysnotions.com